What the critics say about
Pamela Acheson's
THE BEST OF THE BRITISH VIRGIN ISLANDS

"If you want to see the <u>real</u> British Virgin Islands, this book is for you...offers a near-guarantee of a great trip."
—*Independent Publisher*

"*The Best of the British Virgin Islands* is essential to getting the most out of any trip to the British Virgin Islands."
—*Midwest Book Review*

"Pamela Acheson shares her intimate knowledge of hotels, inns, bars, restaurants, shops and attractions."
—*Virgin Islands Weekly Journal*

"Unquestionably the best guidebook ever written on the British Virgin Islands."
—*Peter Island Morning Sun*

"Insider tips and travel secrets."
—*Islands Magazine*

Books by Pamela Acheson and Richard B. Myers

The Best of St. Thomas and St. John, U.S. Virgin Islands
The Best Romantic Escapes in Florida, Volume One
The Best Romantic Escapes in Florida, Volume Two

THE BEST OF THE BRITISH VIRGIN ISLANDS

Third Edition

PAMELA ACHESON

TWO THOUSAND THREE ASSOCIATES
TTTA

Published by
TWO THOUSAND THREE ASSOCIATES
4180 Saxon Drive, New Smyrna Beach, Florida 32169
Phone: 1.800.598.5256 or 386.427.7876   Fax: 386.423.7523

Printed in the United States of America

Acheson, Pamela.
   The best of the British Virgin Islands / Pamela Acheson . — 3nd
ed.
      p.   cm.
      ISBN 0-892285-04-5
   1. British Virgin Islands—Guidebooks.   I. Title
   F2129.A63   1997
   917.297'2504--dc21   97-44960
                                                   CIP

PHOTO CREDITS
Front Cover: Jamie Holmes. Deadman's Beach on Peter Island looking toward Tortola.
Back Cover: Jamie Holmes. Sandy Cay.

ISBN 0-892285-04-5

First Printing May 2003

For Auntie Bea
and for Dick,
for his all-encompassing support, patience,
advice, and editorial contributions.

TABLE OF CONTENTS

"Silver bird fly me away
to where the winter's warm
and the sea breezes
blow through the night"
—*from* Island Blues
by Quito Rhymer

MAPS
The maps in this book are simply meant to be "locator maps" and are provided to show the general location of landmarks, restaurants, hotels, etc. When you arrive in the BVI, you will find excellent, extremely detailed large fold-out maps of the islands that are free and are available at car rental agencies, your hotel, tourist board offices, and elsewhere. If you want detailed maps before your trip, log on to www.caribbean-on-line.com.

ACKNOWLEDGEMENTS
Special thanks to Jon and Paige at Imagecraft and to Juli Maltagliati.

DISCLAIMER
The author has made every effort to ensure accuracy in this book. Neither the author nor the publisher is responsible for anyone's traveling or vacation experiences.

INTRODUCTION

The Best of the British Virgin Islands, Third Edition, is a labor of love. I have been traveling to the Virgin Islands for over 30 years and have been a resident of the British Virgin Islands for much of the past decade.

I have had the pleasure of watching many repeat visitors fall in love with the BVI just the way I did. I wrote this book to try to help every visitor—even the first time visitor—enjoy the very best these wonderful islands have to offer.

You'll notice some special features in the book called "Things people usually wish they had known sooner." Well, in a way, that is what this whole book is all about. I hope my years of island experiences not only offer the very best of the BVI to the reader, but also help everyone avoid the possible pitfalls and problems of traveling to an unfamiliar place.

The book is arranged alphabetically by island, and covers everything, from places to stay to restaurants and snorkel trips. I hope it helps you make educated decisions on everything from where to go, what to do, and how to have the most fun—for you. An appendix in the back of the book provides ferry schedules and other practical information.

The British Virgin Islands are special. I hope when you visit you leave your footprints on dozens of deserted beaches and bring home many special memories.

Enjoy them and have fun!

— P.A.

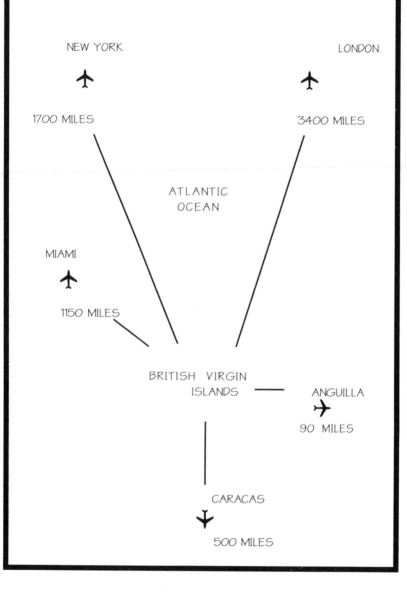

THE BRITISH VIRGIN ISLANDS
IN RELATION TO THE
REST OF THE WORLD

NEW YORK

1700 MILES

LONDON

3400 MILES

ATLANTIC
OCEAN

MIAMI

1150 MILES

BRITISH VIRGIN
ISLANDS

ANGUILLA

90 MILES

CARACAS

500 MILES

1. THE BRITISH VIRGIN ISLANDS

What are they?
They are a stunningly beautiful collection of 50 or so islands, islets, and cays that, with the exception of Anegada, are incredibly close together. Most are mountainous and steep-sided, some are rocky, and many are fringed with white-sand, crescent-shaped beaches. Except for the coral atoll of Anegada, all are volcanic in origin.

Where are they?
In the Caribbean, about 1700 miles southeast of New York City and 1150 miles southeast of Miami. They are 60 miles east of Puerto Rico and about 80 miles slightly northwest of Anguilla. Sombrero, an uninhabited island, sits halfway between the BVI and Anguilla.

Where are the BVI in relation to the USVI?
Right next to each other! The BVI and the USVI share the same archipelago, or group of islands: the USVI have the western half and the BVI the eastern half, with some overlapping in the middle. Some shorelines of the USVI and BVI lie less than half a mile apart.

How are the BVI different from the USVI?
Despite the close shorelines, stepping into the BVI from the USVI is like traveling to a faraway country. The atmosphere is completely different. The USVI population is over 100,000 and two million tourists head there annually. There are stoplights and traffic jams. Only 21,000 people live in all of the BVI. It's an entire country where almost everyone knows everyone else. Resorts are small and there aren't many (there are fewer hotel rooms in the BVI than in the Grand Hyatt Hotel in Manhattan). There is little nightlife. Although the cuisine is delicious, there are only a handful of sophisticated restaurants. The British Virgin Islands are quiet and remote and the U.S. and the USVI seem a million miles away.

What can you do in the BVI?

Walk deserted, dazzling, white-sand beaches. Drive to spectacular mountaintop vistas. Swim, snorkel, and dive in astonishingly clear, calm water. Horseback ride. Hike in the mountains. Sail in exceptionally protected waters. Go deep-sea fishing. Windsurf (locals travel island to island this way!). Or learn to do any of these things. You can also relax, or read, or rest. Or just sit very still and look around you and drink in the view and the soft island breezes. The BVI offer peace, quiet, and a slower pace. The BVI people are warm and friendly. These are the islands to come to for uninhabited beaches. Deserted snorkeling places. Bays where no one else is anchored. This is a place you can take in at your own speed, without crowds of other people blocking your view.

What's special about the BVI?

Everything! One of the BVI's greatest assets is its truly spectacular scenery, above the water and below. There are breathtaking mountaintop panoramas, stunning sunrises and sunsets, beaches that will steal your heart, water in countless unreproducible shades of blue. Below the water line is another magnificent world with great wrecks to dive around and scuba and snorkel areas so full of gaudily decorated fish that it will make you laugh.

Do the islands in the BVI differ from one another?

Absolutely! Despite the fact that the British Virgin Islands are lumped together as the "BVI," each island is actually very different, with its own unique character. When you've seen one, you definitely have not seen them all.

How easy is it to visit several British Virgin Islands?

The BVI is the only place in the entire Caribbean where so many islands are so close together. Many are only three or four miles from each other. Since it's all one country, it's incredibly easy to travel from island to island. Once you've cleared customs into the BVI, you are free to hop from one island to another, without paying departure and arrival taxes, going through customs, or lugging suitcases around. To get from island to island, you can go on a day sail, rent your own little motor boat, or take a public ferry.

2. EACH ISLAND IN A NUTSHELL

All of the British Virgin Islands are hilly and close together except very flat and far-flung Anegada. All are wonderful but each one is unbelievably different from all the others. Each one has a special character all its own.

Anegada is an eleven-mile-long, flat coral atoll surrounded by reefs. It's the northernmost of the BVI and lies barely above sea level about 15 miles north of Virgin Gorda. Only 211 people live on the island. There are very few places to stay and only a handful of extremely simple restaurants but there are miles of deserted beaches, great bonefishing and deep-sea fishing, and some of the best snorkeling in the world.

Beef Island is just 600 feet off Tortola's East End and a short bridge connects the two islands. Beef Island is where the Tortola airport is actually located (which always confuses first-time visitors — "Why am I flying to Beef Island?") and it's also where the ferries leave for Pusser's Marina Cay or Virgin Gorda's North Sound. Beef Island has a nice beach, a windsurfing school, some little stores, several restaurants, some rental villas, and a casual guesthouse.

Cooper Island is five miles south of Tortola. It's a small island favored by the charter yacht crowd because of the large number of available moorings, the calm anchorage, and the popular open-air restaurant. The island also has several inhabitants, some rental villas, and a simple but charming 12-room inn.

Ginger Island is uninhabited and six miles southeast of Tortola.

Great Camanoe Island is just north of Beef Island and has a small number of residents.

13

THE BRITISH VIRGIN ISLANDS

⇧
to Anegada   Necker I.

Mosquito I.

Virgin Gorda

Great Camanoe   Marina C.   Ginger I.

Beef I.   Cooper I.

Guana I.   Salt I.

Tortola

Peter I.

Norman I.

Little Thatch I.

Jost Van Dyke   Great Thatch I.

Great Tobago Island

N

Guana Island is a large and very hilly private island just north of Tortola's East End. The entire island is a remarkable nature preserve and also the setting for a small resort.

Jost Van Dyke is a hilly four-mile-long island five miles northwest of Tortola with 182 inhabitants and beachfront restaurants and bars. Two excellent anchoring harbors (three in the summer when White Bay swells lessen) and Foxy's famous Tamarind Bar make the island a "must stop" for just about everyone visiting the BVI. There are a few places to stay overnight and this island also makes a really great day trip from Tortola.

Little Thatch is small, hilly, and privately owned but there is a little beachfront honeymoon cottage for rent.

Marina Cay is an islet just north of Beef Island and is home to tiny Pusser's Marina Cay Resort, Pusser's Marina Cay Restaurant, and Pusser's Company Store, plus 35 moorings just offshore.

Mosquito Island is a half-mile-square island that is privately owned and borders North Sound just north of Virgin Gorda. The island has several lovely beaches and is very hilly.

Necker Island is a luxurious private retreat a mile and a half north of Virgin Gorda.

Norman Island is five miles south of Tortola and is uninhabited (except for several herds of goats). It's a favorite anchoring spot and features two restaurants, one on the beach and one floating offshore. Some of the BVI's best snorkeling is just off this island.

Peter Island is a four-and-a-half-mile-long, private island five miles south of Tortola with a 52-room resort nestled against its north shore. Ferry service is available from just outside Road Town for those wishing to use the beaches or dine there.

Saba Rock is a spit of an islet just 200 yards offshore of Virgin Gorda in North Sound. This tiny bit of land sports an eight-room resort, a popular restaurant, a large gift shop, and a number of moorings.

15

Salt Island is four miles south of Tortola and its salt ponds were once the BVI's source of salt. Older residents remember boating here to pick up the family's salt supply, necessary for preserving food. A family still lives here but there are no public facilities.

Scrub Island is a bit east of Great Camanoe and has just a few residents and a small restaurant.

Tortola, which is geographically in the center of the BVI, is also the largest, the hilliest, and by far the most populated island, with 17,232 people. Although quiet by U.S. standards, this is the busiest island in the BVI and has the BVI's only real town, Road Town. Stores, bars, restaurants, pubs, and places to stay are clustered in Road Town and also scattered around the island. There are beautiful beaches along the north shore and miles of roads that are astonishingly steep in places but show off awesome views.

Virgin Gorda lies about eight miles east of Tortola, is physically a third smaller, and has a population of only 3,174. The island has one big mountain in the middle that separates two long and slender ends. Although one road crosses over the mountain, the two ends are really two separate destinations, each with its own small number of resorts, shops, and restaurants as well as beautiful beaches. Virgin Gorda's southern section decends into a flat and fairly arid tip with giant boulders scattered about. This is the location of the famous Baths. The northern end of Virgin Gorda, along with the shores of several smaller islands, almost completely encircles calm North Sound, creating an exceptionally protected body of water that is excellent for water sports. Four resorts, three right on Virgin Gorda and one on an islet, and all but one accessible only by boat, are scattered around the hilly North Sound shores.

George Dog, Fallen Jerusalem, and Round Rock are the delightful names of some of the BVI's uninhabited islands. Many have stunning beaches and snorkeling spots which you can reach easily by renting a powerboat or joining a group trip. Keep an eye out for the descriptive names of points and bays, such as the "Inaccessibles" on Mosquito Island or "Cow Wreck Beach" on Anegada.

3. ANEGADA

Pelican Point

Loblolly Bay

Jack Bay

White Bay

Soldier Point

The Settlement

Windlass Bay

Bone Bay

Flamingo Pond

Cow
Wreck
Bay

Setting Point

Pomato Point

Ruffling Point

N

ANEGADA

Anegada is a flat coral atoll 16 miles north of Virgin Gorda which is almost entirely surrounded by treacherous reefs. Snorkelers and divers love Anegada but it definitely can be a sailor's nightmare. There are well over 300 wrecks just offshore. In fact, although the channels are better marked than they used to be, charter companies don't allow their boats to be taken to Anegada without a captain. The approach to the anchorages takes a great deal of skill and local knowledge.

There are just a few places to stay, including a small hotel, a guest house, and a villa. There are a number of very simple restaurants, and miles of stunning white-sand beach. The island itself is not much to look at, but the underwater scenery is spectacular. Exquisite coral formations shimmering with colorful fish begin just inches from shore. You can snorkel here in very calm, clear water and you can swim to one coral grouping after another, for hours and hours. Anegada is also a place to come for excellent deep-sea fishing and bonefishing.

Staying on Anegada is a remarkably relaxing experience. There is "nothing" to do here. Take a picnic to a deserted area of beach or have lunch at a little beach restaurant. Spend the day snorkeling, or kayaking, or perhaps snoozing with a book in your lap. See if you can spot the elusive Anegada rock iguana. Or look for pink flamingoes in the salt ponds (there are over 50 of these marvelous birds now living on Anegada). In the evening catch a stunning sunset and then dine on delicious local lobster. At night, spend hours looking up at the canopy of glittering stars.

If for some reason you develop " island fever" you can always take a day trip over to Tortola.

GETTING TO ANEGADA
Clair Aero Services (*495.2271*) flies between Beef Island/Tortola and the little Anegada airstrip on Mondays, Wednesdays, Fridays, and Sundays. Flights leave Beef Island at 8 am and 5 pm and leave Anegada at 8:20 am and 5:20 pm. The round-trip fare is $66 per person and the flight takes about 10 minutes. **Virgin Gorda Charter Services** (*495.6666*) sometimes has a scheduled ferry boat service between Virgin Gorda's North Sound and Anegada.

GETTING TO ANEGADA FOR THE DAY

Anegada is also a wonderful destination for a day trip. **Fly BVI** (*495.1747*) offers a package trip for $125 per person, minimum of two, that includes a tour of the island and lunch at a beach bar. The flight schedule for **Clair Aero Services** (*see page 18*) also works well for a full day on Anegada. For boat trips to Anegada see Boat Trips from Tortola (*page 73*), Boat Trips from Virgin Gorda (*pages 111 and 124*), or call **Speedy's** (*495.5240*) or **Virgin Gorda Charter Services** (*495.6666*) which sometimes runs a scheduled ferry service between Virgin Gorda's North Sound and Anegada.

GETTING AROUND

Tony's Taxi (*495.8027*) will take you on a tour around the island or drop you at a beach. **ABC Car Rentals** (*495.9466*) rents jeeps for about $60 a day or about $360 a week.

RESTAURANTS

Anegada Reef Hotel Restaurant (*495.8002*), at Setting Point, cooks up outstanding grilled lobster, chicken, ribs, steak, and fish dinners which are served by candlelight. Drop by at lunch for a great lobster salad or a burger or a sandwich. *BLD $$*

Big Bamboo (*495.2019*) is right on beautiful Loblolly Bay beach near Jack Bay Point. It's the place to come for a sweet Anegada lobster, Jamaican jerk chicken, and local conch or grilled snapper. *L (D on request) $$*

Cow Wreck Beach Bar and Grill (*495.9461*), beachfront at Lower Cow Wreck Beach, serves lobster salad sandwiches, conch fritters, and burgers at lunch and fish, ribs, and lobster at dinner. *LD $$*

Dotsy's Bakery and Sandwich Shop (*495.9667*), in the Settlement, bakes breads, muffins, pies, and cookies and serves burgers, fish and chips, and pizza. *Open 9 am-7 pm.*

Flash of Beauty (*495.8014*) is a simple beach bar at Loblolly Bay East serving fresh Anegada lobster, grilled fish, and sandwiches. *Open 10 am-9 pm.*

Neptune's Treasure (*495.9439*), near Setting Point, features dinners of local lobster, swordfish, tuna, and conch at this simple, indoor spot. At lunch, dine on burgers or sandwiches, or select anything from the dinner menu. *BLD $$*

Pomato Point (*495.9466*), right at Pomato Point, offers al fresco dining on a covered terrace. Dine on ribs, chicken, fish, conch, or local lobster. *LD $$*

19

SHOPPING

Anegada Reef Hotel Boutique (*495.8002*) showcases stylish resortwear, local spices and relishes, island prints, original soaps, and excellent gift items.

Pam's Kitchen and Bakery (*495.9237*) bakes breads, muffins, pies, cookies, rolls, and even pizza. Salsas, hot sauces, jams, and soaps are for sale, too. Come by in the morning for hot cinnamon buns.

Pat's Pottery and Art (*495.8031*) features mugs, plates and platters, pitchers, and bowls, all whimsically hand-painted in pastel colors.

BONEFISHING, FLY-FISHING, AND DEEP-SEA FISHING

Cast from the beach or get a kayak for tarpon, snook, and jacks. Or take a day trip with a local guide and reel in a gamefish. **Anegada Reef Hotel** (*495.8002*) offers bonefishing trips. A half-day is $275.

WHERE TO STAY

Anegada Reef Hotel is the island's only hotel and it is very informal and delightfully laid back. If the bartender is not around, you make a drink and write down what you had. Meal hours, special trips, and messages are casually scribbled on a blackboard daily. Rooms are on the spare side, but comfortable. The hotel is on a strand of sand on the south side of the island, but snorkelers and beach lovers will want to spend their days on the deserted and gorgeous beach that runs for miles along the island's spectacular north shore. *20 rooms. Rates for two people, including meals: $250-$275 a night plus 15% service charge and 7% government tax ($215-$250 off-season). Tel: 284.495.8002. Fax: 284.495.9362. Web: www.anegadareef.com*

Lavenda Breeze is Anegada's only real villa. It sits all by itself on the north coast of Anegada, on beautiful Loblolly Bay. The beach plus swimming and snorkeling are right out your door. There are three bedrooms, a fully-equipped kitchen, a comfortable deck that wraps completely around the house, satellite TV, and a VCR. Full provisioning can be arranged. *Weekly rates: $2,800 ($2,000 off-season) 1-4 people; $3,500 ($2,500 off-season) 5-6 people plus 13% service charge and 7% government tax. Tel: 888.868.0199. Fax: 845.255.2452. Web: www.lavendabreeze.com*

Neptune's Treasure, on the south side of the island between Pomato Point and Setting Point, has simple air-conditioned rooms on a narrow strip of beach. *9 rooms. Rates: $105 a night plus 5% for maid service (on request) plus 7% government tax for two people ($90 off-season). Tel/fax: 284.495.9439. Web: www.islandsonline.com/neptunes/index.html*

SNORKELING HINTS

❑When you are snorkeling, never ever touch anything. Sea urchins (those round, black things with thin, black spikes sticking up) and certain corals can sting badly.

❑Also, never ever stand on anything but sand. Coral reefs are exceptionally fragile and grow incredibly slowly. What you destroy with a single crunch of your flipper will take years to replace.

❑To really see what is going on around a reef, try to hover and stare at one particular section. At first you may notice just a few things. But keep looking. The longer you look at one spot, the more activity you'll see.

❑If your mask keeps fogging up, rinse it in the sea water, spit onto the inside, rub the spit all around the glass, rinse the mask briefly, and put it back on. Or buy a defogger (but the spit works equally well and you are less likely to run out).

❑If you forgot your prescription mask (or didn't even know you could get one), you can buy them in the BVI at almost any dive shop.

21

SNORKELING

The waters around the BVI look incredibly peaceful. But stick your head below the surface and you'll see that there's an amazing amount of stuff going on down there.

Even if you don't really like to swim, consider snorkeling in the BVI at least once. The water is astonishingly clear, there are great shipwrecks to explore, and the millions of brightly-colored fish are amazing to see.

Trying to point out the best snorkeling places in the BVI would be sort of like trying to list good French restaurants in Paris. The waters around the British Virgin Islands are teeming with fish—everywhere, right up to the very shoreline.

In fact, if you stand anywhere along the water's edge and drop in broken up bits of stale rolls, it will only be a minute or two before fish will show up to eat. Sometimes the fish will nibble right out of your hand!

How to Snorkel

Snorkeling is something even the most timid soul can try. You can just wade in from the beach with a snorkel and mask and stick your head underwater. Most beaches have excellent snorkeling areas at one or both ends, or wherever a reef has grown. You can also go on organized snorkeling trips all

IN THE BVI

over the BVI. The truly decadent snorkelers simply lie down on one of those brightly-colored yellow floats and stick their head over the edge!

Snorkeling Over Sand
You can snorkel almost anywhere, and beginners are sometimes most comfortable just wading into calm water from the beach and snorkeling over the sand. You'll get to see some fish and you can look for rays, which are the color of the sand and almost impossible to see unless they decide to move. You can also look for turtles and sand dollars.

Snorkeling Over Reefs
The most colorful sea creatures cluster around reefs. It's here that you will see fish, some much smaller than an inch, in all manner of gaudy costumes: bold white and orange stripes, bright purple speckled with silver stars, iridescent stripes of blue and chartreuse. But it's not just the reef fish that are colorful. So is the reef. Watch for the many types of coral. Look for sponges and sea anemones and starfish. And look around you in the water. A great sight to catch is a family of baby squid, each less than half an inch in length, hanging still in a perfect row.

Great Reefs and Great Snorkeling Trips
You can find colorful reefs just offshore of virtually every BVI beach. Or you can take a boat trip to a great snorkeling spot (*see pages 73, 111, and 124*).

VISITING THE USVI FOR A DAY

The USVI and the BVI are right next to each other and yet so very different. It can be fun to head to St. John or St. Thomas for the day. Don't forget your passport!

ST. JOHN

The shoreline of St. John is just a few miles south of Tortola's West End It's a pleasant 40-minute boat ride and you get a chance to explore a completely different island. St. John is mostly a national park. You can hike trails that lead to beautiful beaches and to petroglyphs, wander around the tiny town of Cruz Bay, and browse through little Mongoose Junction, one of the prettiest shopping complexes in the Caribbean. Ferries leave West End, Tortola at 9:15 am and you can come back as late as 5 pm on Friday, 4 pm on Sunday, or 3:30 pm the other days. The round-trip fare is $35. Call Inter-Island Boat Services (*495.4166*).

ST. THOMAS

St. Thomas is only four miles west of the West End of Tortola and you can take a ferry to downtown Charlotte Amalie where there are many shops and restaurants. On Tortola, ferries leave from Road Town and West End. Fares are $44 round-trip from either place. Call Smith's Ferry (*495.4495*) or Native Son (*495.4617*) for schedules. The boat ride takes about 45 minutes from West End to downtown St. Thomas. Speedy's (*495.5240*) also makes the run between the Valley in Virgin Gorda and downtown St. Thomas but it's an hour and a half each way. On Saturdays you can leave at 8:30 am and catch the 3:30 pm ferry back.

4. COOPER

Quart-a-Nancy Point

Coral Bay

COOPER ISLAND
BEACH CLUB
& RESTAURANT

Dustry Point

Great
Snorkeling

Hallover Bay

Markoe Bay

⇧ N

COOPER

Cooper Island is a small but hilly island that has long been popular with the charter boat crowd. There's a little beach and some outstanding snorkeling. There's also a casual restaurant, a nice little barefoot bar, a boutique, a dive shop, some rental houses (www.cooperisland.com), and a little resort. And that's it! There are no roads or cars on this island and only about six people live here.

The Cooper Island Beach Club is a great getaway. Even though it's isolated, every night you can meet a new group of people at the bar who have anchored for the night. It's kind of fun to be a "local" and watch people come and go. If you want to visit Tortola for the day, hop on the ferry any weekday morning (see schedule page 138). Each week on season there is a scheduled trip to Virgin Gorda. If you want to come just for the day rent a boat or take a boat trip (see pages 73,111, 124).

Cooper Island Restaurant (*VHF Channel 16*) has been here for years. It's an informal open-air place which looks out over the bay. For lunch you can get hamburgers, conch fritters, soup and salad, a grilled vegetable sandwich, and superb ratatouille (luckily, the ratatouille is also offered as an appetizer for dinner). Evening specialties include barbecue chicken breast, conch creole, grilled mahi mahi, and penne pasta with chicken or shrimp. The bar is truly barefoot, and it's open all day. *LD (continental breakfast for hotel guests) $$*

The **Cooper Island Beach Club** is a very compact but surprisingly private place that is ultra-casual, quite relaxing, and slightly like camping. Six duplex West-Indian style yellow cottages are hidden among the palm trees just 50 feet from a little beach. All units are on the second floor (the first floor is storage and cistern) and views look out through tropical foliage. Units are small and modestly furnished, but appealing. All have little kitchens with gas stoves, outdoor showers, ceiling fans (no air conditioning), tape decks, and balconies. Water is from rain stored in the cistern (use it sparingly). There is no electricity plant on the island and lights, ceiling fans, and tape deck (bring your favorites) are powered by a 12 volt DC set-up in each room (a 110 volt outlet can be used to power up batteries in the evening when the generator is on). Shorts, T-shirts, and bathing suit are all you'll need. Bring groceries from Road Town or request provisioning. Assistant Manager Curt Berkley is always around and extremely helpful. *12 rooms. General Manager: Chris Tillings. Rates: $175 plus 17% tax and service per night for two people ($115 spring, fall; $95 summer). Reservations: 800.542.4624. Tel: 284.495.9084. Web: www.cooper-island.com*

26

HELPFUL HINTS

❑On the BVI, as on many islands, people exchange greetings and inquire about each other's health before getting down to business. This is true whether they run into a friend, stop for gas, go to the grocery store, or order food from a waitress. It's considered very rude to skip this conversational step. So start with a "Hello, how are you doing today?" and have a little introductory conversation. (Actually you'll find this "politeness" is appreciated stateside also.)

❑In these islands, when you didn't hear what someone said, the polite way to ask for a repeat is to say "Say again?" or "Please repeat" rather than "What?"

❑It may puzzle you that sometimes you can't always understand the British Virgin Islanders even though they are speaking English. This is not just because of the West Indian accent. It is also because the idioms are different. In the states, you "go for a swim," didn't "hear" something, "turn" a latch, "put" it down, say "Yes." Islanders "take a sea bath," didn't "catch" something, "swing" a latch, "rest" it, and say "It would seem so." A list of all the idiomatic differences would fill a book.

❑Most islanders are actually going out of their way to talk "your language" when they talk to you. They are speaking extra slowly and avoiding the local phrases that seem to most confuse visitors. (Try listening to a group of islanders chatting among themselves and you'll see how much faster and more idiomatically they talk.) Also, the accent varies from Jost to Tortola to Virgin Gorda.

THINGS PEOPLE USUALLY WISH THEY HAD KNOWN SOONER

❑**Bugs.** Keep a little container of bug repellant (like a Cutter stick) with you *at all times*. This is actually a good idea if you are traveling anywhere in the Caribbean. It's not that any place is always buggy, it just can be buggy practically anywhere when there is absolutely no breeze.

❑**Itchy bug bites.** If you get bitten and have nothing to stop the itch, remember that a dab of straight gin or vodka usually works (you're supposed to apply it directly to the bite, but some people swear it works just as well if you drink it instead).

❑**Soap but no water.** When you are in a washroom in the BVI (or, in fact, almost anywhere in the Caribbean), check that water will actually come out of the faucet before you put that liquid soap on your hands. It's tough to get it all off if there's no water around. (It can be handy to carry Wash & Dries with you.)

❑**Missing meals.** If you are flying from the states to the BVI via Puerto Rico, you will discover that connections often make it impossible to eat for many hours, so tuck some food and a bottle of water in your carry-on.

❑**Holidays.** On major public holidays (*see Appendix*), almost everything in the BVI closes up.

❑**ATM machines.** Most BVI banks have them but they rarely work, so don't count on getting cash this way.

5. GUANA

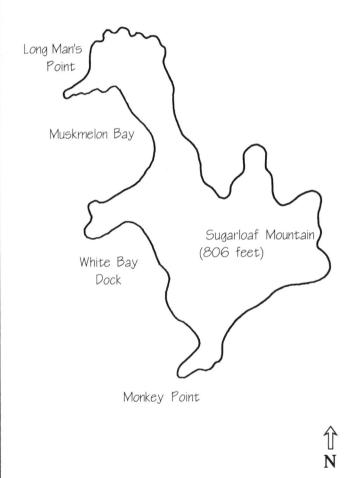

Long Man's
Point

Muskmelon Bay

White Bay
Dock

Sugarloaf Mountain
(806 feet)

Monkey Point

N

GUANA

*Guana, at 850 acres, is the seventh largest British Virgin Island. It is extremely hilly and very private and home to the **Guana Island** resort. All of the island is a nature preserve and wildlife and bird sanctuary and there are rare roseate flamingos, masked boobys, and frigate birds, and many kinds of herons. At least 50 species of birds are regularly found there. Scientists from several academic institutions are engaged in on going studies of Guana Island's flora and fauna.*

Peaceful paths meander through lush tropical greenery and brilliant flowering bushes and trees. There are seven usually empty beaches and lots of hiking trails (some quite strenuous) that go all over the island. Staying here is a one-of-a-kind experience. It is simple, civilized, and very relaxing. The island is truly private. The dining room and other facilities are not open to outside guests and there are no day-trippers on the island (except sometimes at the beaches—all beaches in the BVI are public).

The **Guana Island** resort is perched on the top of one of Guana Island's hills and there are astonishingly beautiful panoramic views in every direction. Appealing rooms, most in cottages with handsome stone walls and beamed ceilings, are simply decorated but very comfortable. Many have separate sitting areas and all have large porches or balconies and very private entrances. Breakfast, lunch, and dinner are served on stone terraces. Guests gather in the drawing room for before-dinner cocktails and after-dinner cognacs. Dinner is a casually elegant affair with a number of courses and guests generally dine together at several large tables and join in the evening conversation.

There are seven beautiful and usually deserted beaches, a little honor beach bar, good snorkeling areas, tennis courts, and various water activities and therapeutic massage (in your room or on the beach) are available. Hiking trails lead to beaches and secluded vistas. You can spend days hiking and swimming or reclined on the beach or your private terrace absorbed in a book or just taking in the views. This can be a remarkably relaxing place. *15 units. General Managers: Roger Miller and Bridget MacArthur. Rates (all meals, house wines with lunch and dinner, and use of all equipment): $850 for two people ($640 off-season). North Beach Cottage $1,500 ($1,200 off-season) plus 17% tax and service. Closed Sept., Oct. Reservations: 800.544.8262. Tel: 914.967.6050. Fax: 914.967.8048. Local Tel: 284.494.2354. Web: www.guana.com*

DID YOU KNOW?

❏If you pushed all the British Virgin Islands together into one land mass, it would only cover 59 square miles. That's about the same size as Nantucket Island. Or one twentieth the size of Rhode Island, the smallest state in the union.

❏William Thornton, who designed the U.S. Capitol building, was born in the BVI in 1759 on the island of Jost Van Dyke.

❏Only about 21,000 people live in the BVI. Seven times this number of people live in Stamford, Connecticut. And twice this many people live in Beverly Hills, California. If everybody in the BVI (the whole entire country) took a seat in the 80,000-seat New Orleans Superdome, well...there would still be 59,000 empty seats!

❏Latitudinally, the BVI are located roughly half-way between the equator and New York City.

❏It's only about 10 degrees warmer in the summer than in the winter in the BVI. Winter temperatures average about 75 degrees, summer about 85 degrees.

❏If you headed directly east from the BVI, you would eventually be in the Sahara Desert. As a matter of fact, in the BVI in the summer the air is sometimes hazy because it is full of Sahara dust, fine particles of sand that have been blown by the trade winds all the way from Africa. You can actually feel a fine layer of grittiness on the surface of things.

❑The wind in the BVI generally blows in the opposite direction from the winds that sweep across the United States and Europe. On these continents, the wind and the weather generally come from the west. In the BVI, the wind and the weather generally come out of the east.

❑The BVI really does have seasons. Although it rarely ever rains for long, in the winter there are more frequent two-minute cloudbursts (which keep the hills emerald green), the humidity is low, and there are very steady trade winds. Summer is frequently dry (the hills can turn brown), more humid, and less windy. It can also be hazy when a tropical wave is passing through.

❑The Christmas winds, which usually start (you guessed it) just around Christmas, are strong and sometimes stay at 30 to 40 knots for several days.

❑The flat road on Tortola that runs between Road Town and West End wasn't built until 1966 when they reclaimed that flat land from the sea. As recently as 1965 it was an all-day trip by donkey from that end of the island to town! You'll still catch sight of old-timers traveling the old-fashioned way!

6. JOST VAN DYKE

Green Cay

Pelican Cay

Little Jost Van Dyke

Sandy Cay

East End Harbour

Little Harbour

Great Harbour

White Bay

West End
Point

N

JOST VAN DYKE IN A NUTSHELL

Jost Van Dyke is about five miles northwest of Tortola. It's four miles long, very hilly, and home to just 182 people. The island is known by yachters around the world for its gentle anchorages and for its delightful barefoot, beachfront bars, including the famous Foxy's, which is one of the most celebrated watering holes in the entire Caribbean.

Four tiny settlements are tucked along Jost's curvy southern and eastern shores: White Bay, Great Harbour, Little Harbour, and East End. A single road connects the settlements and then turns into a roller coaster-like heart-stopper as it loops up into the hills and over steep peaks.

There are only a few facilities for staying overnight. Most people either catch a ferry or rent a small powerboat and visit for the day or arrive on their own boat or on a charterboat and spend the night on water. Those that do stay on land have the opportunity to be incredibly laid-back and relaxed. There's virtually no contact with the outside world and no need to ever wear shoes, unless you decide to hike the road or the hills. If you get island fever, you can hop on a ferry and go to Tortola for the day.

WHAT YOU CAN DO ON JOST VAN DYKE

You can swim, snorkel, read, rest, bask in the sun, hike the hills, snooze with no interruptions. Restaurants and bars are built right at the edge of the beach and you can walk from one to another in a delightfully relaxed, "no shoes required" atmosphere.

GETTING TO JOST VAN DYKE FROM TORTOLA AND USVI

Two companies run little ferries between West End, Tortola and Great Harbour, Jost Van Dyke (*see schedule page 138*). These are also the boats that bring supplies to Jost, so you may be sharing a seat with cases of soda and cartons of just about anything. Bear in mind that the boat may leave early or late, so get to the dock with time to spare. When someone begins to untie the lines, that means the boat is leaving, so hop aboard. Ferries also run from the USVI (*see schedule page 138*).

Note: If you are staying on Jost and arriving directly from St. Thomas, USVI you must clear customs at the Customs Office at Great Harbour.

EXPLORING JOST VAN DYKE

The only flat land on Jost Van Dyke is found along several curvy bays on the southern and eastern sides of the island and it is here that people settled, at Great Harbour, Little Harbour, White Bay, and East End Harbour. The island's single road forms a six-mile, curvy loop that runs up and down over seaside hills to connect the shoreline settlements and then heads up across the peaks of the uninhabited part of the island to show off stunning views. Driving this road is a delightful adventure.

Between the settlements, the road is mostly paved and, although quite steep in places, is easily driveable. However, the section of road that takes off into the mountains is very rough (it's sometimes crushed rock, sometimes dirt, and occasionally grass), breathtakingly steep, and contains some unforgettable hairpin turns. It also provides spectacular views of the shoreline below and of sea and nearby islands as it twists and turns across virgin hills, so be sure to bring a camera. This long section of the road is little traveled and it is rare to encounter another car or even to see another person.

If you prefer not to take the whole road, there is a shortcut up to it just to the west of Rudy's Suprette. When you get to the top, turn left for the short version, and right for the long. If you want to leave the driving to someone else, hire a taxi for a tour.

You can take taxis between the settlements. Hardy souls can walk from Great Harbour to White Bay. It takes a good 15 minutes just to get over the hill (a real killer in the afternoon sun) to the very eastern edge of White Bay beach and it's another 10 minutes along the sand and over some rocks to the beach bars at the western end of White Bay.

Renting a jeep
You can rent a jeep from Sendrick Chinnery at **Paradise Jeep Rentals** (*495.9477 or 496.8200*) for about $50 a day.

Hiring a taxi
Bun (*499.8871*), Steve (*499.4361, 495.9487*), Greg (*499.5127, 495.9401*) and Abe (*495.9327*) drive taxis. Look for them by the Great Harbour Dock or near the Customs House or call (there's a pay phone near the Customs House). The fare from Great Harbour to White Bay or Little Harbour is about $5 per person.

35

Renting a dinghy or a boat

Steve at **Sharkie's Dinghy Rentals** (*495.9487 or 495.4631*) rents dinghies for about $60 per day plus fuel. Dave (*495.9538*) rents dinghies and also 200 hp boats that you can take to nearby islands or even St. John, USVI.

Hiring a water taxi

Steve (*495.9487 or 495.4631*) will take you in his 26' Bertram water taxi to or from other islands. Greg (*495.9401*) also provides water taxi service between islands. The rate to or from St. Thomas, USVI is about $175.

AREAS TO VISIT

Great Harbour, Little Harbour, and White Bay are the the three areas of the island that have bars, restaurants, and shops and this next section describes each area separately. However, because there are so few places to stay on the island, all are grouped together and described beginning on page 42. Bear in mind that even though Jost is an extremely casual island, you must make dinner reservations by late afternoon. Supplies on the island are quite limited and if they know you are coming, they can speed off to another island and get additional food if necessary.

GREAT HARBOUR

Great Harbour, the most populated area of Jost Van Dyke, is a very small settlement, with casual bar-restaurants and shops scattered near the shore. The public dock, where the ferries tie up, is on the west side of the harbour and you can walk or taxi the short distance along the shore to "town." The water is good for swimming and snorkeling, but watch out for dinghies speeding about. By the way, when you are on the beach at Great Harbour looking out across the water, virtually all the distant hills you see are part of St. John (USVI).

```
                    GREAT  HARBOUR
                        □  Ice House
                        □  Christine's Bakery
                        □  Nature's Basket
  Rudy's  Club   Ali Baba  Customs      Ice Cream, Groceries
    □   □Paradise □      Office      □Wendells World   Foxy's □
                          □
  ↙ to Ferry Dock                               Foxy's Dock
```

GREAT HARBOUR SHOPPING

Christine's Bakery (*495.9281*) showcases delicious breads and rolls including coconut and banana bread, brownies, cakes, pies, and doughnuts—all freshly baked, plus her irresistible cinnamon and raisin sweet rolls.

Foxy's Boutique (*495.9275*) looks petite from the beach but inside you'll find one room keeps leading to another, and all are stocked with soft cotton dresses, casual resortwear, colorful T-shirts and swimwear and shorts for the whole family, cassette tapes and CDs of island music (including Foxy's, naturally), books, postcards, sunscreen, batteries, a variety of unusual gift items, and a full line of Foxy's products, from playing cards to boxer shorts.

Ice House (*495.9263*), which is at the end of the little road that goes past Christine's, is the place to go for ice—by the cube and by the block. Be sure to stop here for a bottle of Joyce Chinnery's outstanding mango chutney.

Jost Van Dyke Groceries (*no phone*), is tucked in the back corner of this West Indian cottage (locally referred to as the mini-mall), across from Wendell's. Shelves are jammed with everything from batteries to bottles of Pinot Grigio.

Jost Van Dyke Ice Cream Parlor (*no phone*) offers ice cream in an assortment of flavors. It's at the front of the "mini-mall" across from Wendell's.

Nature's Basket (*495.9312*), next to Christine's, features exquisite seasonal fruits grown up in the hills on Jost Van Dyke. Come here for deliciously sweet pineapples, papayas, mangoes, and bananas. You'll also find a small selection of fresh vegetables, cheeses, eggs, canned goods, and sodas.

Rudy's Suprette (*495.9282*), at the opposite end of the beach from Foxy's, carries canned goods, bottled water, sodas, crackers, beer, and a variety of miscellaneous items which change depending on what the supply boat delivers. If you are looking for almost anything, there's a chance you'll find it here.

"It was supposed to be open for only one day, for the Harvest Festival in 1967."

— Foxy Callwood,
smiling as he commented on his famous Tamarind Bar,
which he has now kept open for almost 40 years!

GREAT HARBOUR RESTAURANTS AND BARS

Ali Baba's (*495.9280*) offers burgers, conch fritters, and rotis plus an inviting bar. Don't miss the Monday night all-you-can-eat pig roast. *BLD $$*

Christine's Bakery (*495.9281*) is the place to come for breakfast. Sit on the terrace and dine on eggs and bacon, fresh fruit, freshly-baked coconut bread, or Christine's exceptional cinnamon and raisin sweet rolls. *BLD $*

Club Paradise (*495.9267*) features excellent black bean soup, cheeseburgers, and West Indian specialties like conch stew for lunch, and fresh fish and steak for dinner. Sometimes there is a pig roast on Wednesday nights. Dinner can seem a bit hectic, but the staff manages well and keeps on smiling. *LD $$*

Foxy's Tamarind Bar (*495.9258*) serves some of the very best food on the island and gallons and gallons of their irresistible painkiller punch, but the real draw here is Foxy himself, who is never without his guitar. He sings most afternoons (except for Sunday or if he's gone fishing) and wanders in and out other times, always happy to create impromptu, amusing ballads about his guests. Come here for a cold bottle of Foxy's own beer plus burgers, lobster salad sandwiches, lasagna, and rotis for lunch, and grilled fresh fish, steak, and lobster for dinner. Barbecues are Friday and Saturday evenings. Despite the immense popularity of this place, the atmosphere remains remarkably unhurried and pleasant, thanks to Foxy's wife, Tessa, and to the exceptionally professional staff. Check out the business cards stapled almost everywhere. Find anyone you know? *No food Sept. but bar is often open and you might find Foxy. LD $$*

Rudy's Mariner's Rendezvous Restaurant (*495.9282*), at the western edge of Great Harbour, has a popular bar and also serves everything from burgers to lobster. *BLD $$*

Wendell's World (*495.9259*) is a casual spot for burgers, sandwiches, and fried chicken. *LD $$*

GREAT HARBOUR NIGHTLIFE

Foxy's Tamarind Bar (*495.9258*). Foxy himself entertains most afternoons (except Sundays). Live bands play Thursday, Friday, and Saturday nights (and often on Tuesday and Wednesday nights, on season). Some weekday nights a DJ takes over. To find out what band is playing when you are visiting, pick up the current edition of the *Limin' Times* or go online to www.limin-times.com.

Club Paradise (*495.9267*). A steel band sometimes plays Wednesday evenings.

LITTLE HARBOUR

Little Harbour, a tiny settlement, is separated from Great Harbour by a large hill. It's a popular anchorage but there is virtually no beach. Several ultra-casual restaurants are right at the water's edge.

LITTLE HARBOUR SHOPPING

Sidney's Peace & Love (*495.9271*) has an outdoor boutique and sells cotton dresses, T-shirts, and more.

Abe's Little Harbour (*495.9329*) has a little grocery inside.

LITTLE HARBOUR RESTAURANTS AND BARS

Abe's Little Harbour (*495.9329*), in a cottage on the eastern edge of the harbour, turns out delicious lobster, chicken, fish, conch, and spareribs for lunch and dinner and holds a pig roast Wednesday night in season. *BLD $$*

Harris' Place (*495.9295*), painted pastel blue and purple, serves meals at picnic tables at the water's edge and cooks up full breakfasts plus hamburgers and sandwiches for lunch and West Indian-style fish and conch and lobster for dinner. There's a pig roast nightly in season. Call Cynthia to make a reservation for dinner. *BLD $$*

Sidney's Peace & Love (*495.9271*), with an eclectic variety of tables spread across the dock out over the water and under a makeshift roof (which also serves as the display rack for a large display of T-shirts) prepares breakfast daily and lobster, chicken, fish, and West Indian dishes for lunch and dinner. *BLD $$*

LITTLE HARBOUR NIGHTLIFE

Sidney's Peace & Love (*495.9271*). Bands perform here sometimes on season.

Harris' Place. Ruben Chinnery plays his guitar and sings Monday nights.

WHITE BAY

White Bay has two long and lovely beaches, connected by a path that wends its way across an outcropping of rock. On the western beach is tiny Sandcastle Hotel, a handful of beach restaurants and bars, and a few beach boutiques. This is a popular day trip from St. Thomas in the USVI and this end of the beach can actually get extremely crowded on weekend afternoons. East of the rock outcropping, just over the hill from Great Harbour, is Ivan's outstanding Stress-Free Bar, a little campground, and several villas.

WHITE BAY SHOPPING

Sheniques Boutique (*no phone*), on the beach west of Sandcastle, sells delightful island wear: colorful men's shirts, gauzy dresses, sarongs, T-shirts.

Ivan's Stress-Free Bar (*495.9358*) rents snorkel equipment and has a selection of used paperback books.

Sandcastle Resort Boutique (*495.9888*) features T-shirts, bathing suits, film, suntan lotion, and postcards.

Wendell's World Boutique (*no phone*) carries clothing, beachwear, and gifts.

White Bay Grocery Shop (*no phone*), outlined in shells, carries numerous items, from potato chips to suntan lotion to cans of tuna to cold sodas and juices.

WHITE BAY RESTAURANTS, BARS, AND NIGHTLIFE

Gertrude's Beach Bar and Restaurant (*495.9104*) is a good choice for a painkiller or an icy cold beer or a frosty frozen concoction, plus burgers and lobster salad for lunch and barbequed ribs or fish for dinner. *LD $$*

Ivan's Stress-Free Bar (*495.9358*) is tucked into the foliage along the eastern section of White Bay beach. There's a sandy veranda, a belly-up bar, and delightful decor: thousands of shells in patterns on the pastel-painted walls and ceiling. Ivan's daughter, Chef Darlene, prepares burgers, tuna melts, grilled cheese and local beef or chicken pates for lunch. Every Thursday evening the locally-famous guitarist Ruben entertains and Ivan throws a cookout barbecue (reservations by 4 pm essential!). Friday nights Elvis from Bequia entertains, and you can say you "saw Elvis on Jost Van Dyke." Ivan's is the home of the International "All Stars Ever-Changing Band." Bring an instrument and join the festive jam session, which can occur almost any night. On some nights you can catch someone famous jamming away. If no one shows up to jam, Ivan entertains solo. *L daily (D Thurs., reservations essential). $-$$*

Sandcastle Restaurant's (*495.9888*) dinner is surprisingly and delightfully elegant, as tablecloths, candlelight, and smooth service magically transform what is known during the day as the Soggy Dollar Bar (*see below*). The four-course menu changes nightly and includes a delicious soup (such as butternut squash), a creative salad, and a tempting dessert plus a choice of three entrees, such as grilled chicken breast with peanut sauce, grilled veal chop with Bordelaise sauce, or braised shrimp. Call after 10 am to find out the day's menu and, please, choose your entree before 4 pm. Dinner begins promptly at 7 pm. *Closed Mon. and Sept. Reservations essential by 4 pm. Prix fixe $32 plus 15%.*

Soggy Dollar Bar (*495.9888*) at the Sandcastle Hotel claims to be the true originator of that smooth rum concoction known as the painkiller (check out the letter on the wall). Dine at lunch in your bathing suit on a juicy hamburger, a great flying fish sandwich, a spicy roti, or tasty conch fritters. Order lunch at the bar and carry it to a table or to the beach or even a hammock. This is also a great place to come for breakfast, which is served from 9:15 to 10 am. There's a morning special for $10 or toast and cereal for $5. It's packed here on Sunday afternoons when Ruben Chinnery strums his guitar and sings his very own renditions of popular ballads and soft rock. *No breakfast Sept. BL $$*

Jewel's Shack (*no phone*) is a tiny place that specializes in burgers, hot dogs, and light snacks during the day. *L $*

41

JOST VAN DYKE LODGING

There are only a handful of places to stay overnight on Jost Van Dyke. A tiny resort, several villas, and a campground are on White Bay. On remote East End you'll find a small collection of villas.

Don't come here looking for luxury. Life on Jost Van Dyke is extremely simple: no traffic, virtually no television, phones that work haphazardly. For those who can bear to be "unplugged" it's an outstandingly relaxing experience. You'll need very few clothes—a bathing suit plus some T-shirts and shorts. There are almost no laundry facilities, most air-conditioning is of the natural kind, water comes mostly from cisterns and must be used sparingly, and although the island was recently electrified, power outages are common.

What you get instead of modern conveniences are a fabulously laid-back atmosphere, nights of extraordinarily brilliant stars, a chance to just sit and watch the scenery change as the sun catches a wave or a sudden cloudburst momentarily obscures a nearby island and creates a staggeringly beautiful rainbow. On Jost Van Dyke you get the chance to really pause.

However, on Jost you are not completely isolated. Great Harbour and Little Harbour are two of the most popular anchorages in the BVI and boaters come ashore to dine. White Bay is hugely popular with day-trippers from the USVI and, especially on season, White Bay bars and beaches can be frenetic in the afternoon.

If you want you can join in the fun, knowing that in a few hours you will once again be experiencing the simplicity and peace of living on a relatively large island with less than 200 other people. If you want to avoid the afternoon crowds you can visit the bubbly pool at East End, hike the road, or have a water taxi drop you off on the beach of a nearby uninhabited island, or even take a day trip to Tortola.

If you really want complete isolation, your best bet is Sandy Ground Estates at East End.

Rates provided here are on season and do not include 7% hotel tax or 10% service charge. Off-season rates are in parentheses.

SANDCASTLE HOTEL

Slip into a state of true laid-backness at this delightful and very tiny beachfront hideaway.

Four hexagonal, simply furnished but quite charming cottages are set in the trees at the edge of lovely White Bay beach and ceiling fans capture the sea breezes. The two Beachfront Cottages have two rooms and the two Garden Cottages have one room. There are also two additional more traditionally-shaped Garden Rooms with air-conditioning. This is the place to come when you want to read, relax, lie in a hammock, snorkel, snooze, make forays around the island, and come back for a quiet candlelit dinner. The location is at the busiest end of the beach, but it's kind of fun to see everyone come and go. The restaurant (*see page 41*) serves all meals and is excellent.

6 units. Daily Rates: Beachfront Cottage $250 ($175), Garden Cottage $200 ($125), Garden Room $220 ($145) for two people not including taxes or meals. Closed Sept. Owners/Managers: Debby Pearse and Bruce Donath. Tel: 284.495.9888. Fax: 284.495.9999. Web: www.sandcastle-bvi.com

JOST VAN DYKE VILLA RENTALS

Note: At villas, linens are provided but you will need to bring absolutely everything else, from salt to charcoal to paper towels, plus food. However, this is actually easy to do (the hardest part is making the perfect list). Whether you arrive from Tortola or St. Thomas (USVI), your taxi driver will stop at a grocery on the way to the ferry. (This is the best bet if you want to choose your vegetables, etc. On Tortola, you may need to stop at several stores to find everything you need.) You can also order in advance on line from www.amplehamper.com and have your provisions waiting at your villa.

PINK HOUSE

Sleep to the sound of lapping waves in this inviting villa just steps from the beach.

Tucked among palm trees at the eastern end of White Bay beach is this comfortable, pink-roofed West Indian-style house. It is about two dozen steps back from the water and is the only house at this end of the beach. On the main level are two bedrooms, two bathrooms, a living room, a fully-equipped kitchen, and a large porch. A third bedroom is on the lower level. The large covered veranda looks out to views of White Bay and nearby islands. There is a charcoal grill, a stereo/CD player, a VCR and TV monitor (no TV reception), and a small collection of videos and books. Rooms are cooled by ceiling fans.

Weekly rates: $1,900 ($1,500 off-season; $2,800 holiday). Manager: Olivia Callwood. Reservations: info@pinkhousebvi.com or 319.533.1281. Web: www.pinkhousebvi.com

WHITE BAY VILLAS

Enjoy dazzling views from this hillside villa complex that sits high above beautiful White Bay.

These villas are built into the steep hillside above the east end of White Bay and the views of sea and neighboring islands are stunning. The three villas built out along the point of the hill are bright white with red tile roofs. The largest is a 4,000-square-foot multi-level house with three bedrooms, three baths, and numerous verandas. Further out on the point are an adjacent two-bedroom and one-bedroom villa that can be combined as one rental. Set back into the hillside are three charming one-bedroom West Indian-style cottages with hip roofs. These cozy cottages have a separate living room and a private veranda. All six villas have fully-equipped kitchens, and are cooled by ceiling fans. There are books, games, videos for the TV/VCR, and a stereo/CD player. A steep path leads right down to the beach for morning swims and nighttime walks.

6 villas. Weekly rates: 3-bedroom villa $3,900 ($3,120), two-bedroom villa $2,900 ($2,320), one-bedroom villa and cottages $1,900 ($1,520). Reservations: Bonnie White at 410.571.6692. Fax: 410.571.6693. Web: www.jostvandyke.com

SANDY GROUND ESTATES

Experience real isolation at these hillside villas on East End.

These eight one-, two-, and three-bedroom houses are tucked here and there in the hillside above a small but lovely beach with a good snorkeling reef at very remote East End. Each has been individually designed and each has a character all its own. One is perched on the rocks. Another is high on the hillside. Some are close to the beach. Houses are built some distance from each other and are extremely private. Many have outstanding views. All have full kitchens and VCRs with TV monitor (no TV reception). If you prefer not to bring supplies, management will stock the house. This villa complex is truly an escape and is very remote. These houses are not within walking distance of a restaurant or store. However, with a bit of a walk, you can get to a place where a taxi can pick you up for day or dinner trips to White Bay, Great Harbour, and Little Harbour.

8 villas. Weekly Rates: $1,950 for two people, $300 for each additional person ($1,400; $200). Tel: 284.494.3391. Fax: 284.495.9379. Web: www.sandyground.com

WHITE BAY CAMPGROUND

Ivan Chinnery, of Ivan's Stress-Free Bar fame, runs this extremely simple campground with four equipped campsites (lamp and bed and ice chest inside a tent) for $35 a night; 10 bare campsites for $15 a night; and eight screened cabins with lamp, bed, and ice chest for $45 to $60 a night. Bathrooms and showers are near. *Tel: 284.495.9312 or 284.495.9358.*

A DAY TRIP TO JOST VAN DYKE

There are three areas to visit: Great Harbour, Little Harbour, and White Bay. Restaurants are casual, open-air, and waterfront. It's very quiet here off-season and places can be closed much of September.

WHAT YOU CAN DO ON JOST VAN DYKE

This is an excellent one-day adventure. It's a 25-30 minute ferry ride from Tortola. You can walk along the beach, swim, snorkel, hike, eat good food, and visit bars in a delightfully relaxed, "no-shoes required" atmosphere.

THE FERRY RIDE FROM TORTOLA

What to bring on a day trip: some cash (not every place takes credit cards), swimsuit, towel, sunscreen, camera, film, snorkel equipment. Bare feet are the norm at restaurants, but bring sturdy shoes if you want to hike the hills or the road.

CATCHING THE FERRY

In the BVI, the ferry to Jost Van Dyke leaves from West End, Tortola (*see schedules page 138*). There are two ferries, the *Paradise Express* and the *When*, so named, many say, because the *When* leaves whenever it's ready. Both ferries are also delivery boats for goods and when they are loaded, they often leave. Departure might be a half hour late, but it can also be 15 minutes early! Get to the dock with time to spare. Locate the ferry (it should be at the left end of the dock as you walk through the dock's entryway). If it's still being loaded, you probably have time to pick up a soda across the street at Zelma's or a beer to go at Uncle Joe's Rocky Willow.

Then go sit somewhere close to the ferry you plan to take and enjoy the sights of the harbor. Those pastel buildings across the water are Pusser's Landing, a Pusser's Store, and shops. Generally, the only indication that the boat is actually leaving is when someone begins to untie the lines. This is your cue to hop aboard. By the way, sometimes you buy a ticket before boarding and sometimes you pay the $12 fare when you get to Jost Van Dyke (there is no ticket office).

GREAT SIGHTS TO SEE FROM THE FERRY

As you leave the dock, watch for the interesting-looking grey house built right into a cliff on the right, on Tortola's point, and the picturesque island across the water on your left. For years the rumor was that the guy who built the grey house also bought this island, which is known as Little Thatch, so he could look across at an unspoiled view! However, Little Thatch is now owned by someone else and can be rented (*see page 56*). Once the boat turns right and you clear passage between Great Thatch (on the left) and Tortola, Jost Van Dyke will be dead ahead and Tortola's north shore will appear on the right. Those two big green "gum drops" of land on Tortola define Smuggler's Cove. Just beyond the further "gum drop" is Long Bay. You can't see Cane Garden Bay, but the distant hill with a long scar of erosion is at its far edge. Approaching Jost Van Dyke, you'll see two tiny islands on the right, each with a brilliant strip of white sand. The one closest to Jost Van Dyke is Green Cay. The other is Sandy Cay and is owned by Laurance Rockefeller. You can also see a strip of road that runs along Jost's hillside. This is the only road on the island.

ARRIVING AT GREAT HARBOUR

The ferry takes you to the public dock on the west side of Great Harbour, the main "town" on Jost Van Dyke. White Bay and Little Harbour can be reached by taxi.

WONDERFUL SIGHTS TO LOOK FOR

Goats in boats. If you think you've lost your mind because you think you see a dinghy full of animals out there, keep looking. It's probably goats. Islanders keep their goats on many of the uninhabited islands, and move them around on occasion, and it is not unusual to catch sight of a Boston Whaler with ten or twelve goats milling around!

Sea turtles. When you are snorkeling or floating or boating, look for big sea turtles. Before a turtle surfaces, it surreptitiously sticks its head out of the water to see what is going on. You can easily mistake it for a drifting stick.

Rays. You can sometimes spot a ray at rest when you are snorkeling over sand. Study the bottom carefully. They lie perfectly still and are almost indistinguishable from the sand.

Rainbows. Brilliant rainbows show up everywhere in the BVI, all day long. Even the briefest rain somewhere in the distance can create a rainbow and you'll get to see it splashed across the sky, radiant in the sunlight.

Double rainbows. The very luckiest people get to see complete double rainbows. Even a partial double is considered good luck.

Hummingbirds. They hang fluttering in the air close to flowering bushes, in glistening greens and blues.

FERRYING AROUND

Ferries are an extremely pleasant way to travel around the BVI or to visit St. John or St. Thomas in the USVI. Many ferries have at least some open-air seating. Usually you can sit outside and watch the scenery. You'll get a lot of sun here, but the air is nice and the views are just wonderful. Even if a brief shower comes by, you'll be dry before you reach your destination. Do check the seas. If they are rough, it can be splashy on the windward side. You can catch a ferry in the late afternoon or you can also stay for dinner and head home after dark (*see page 72*)—a nighttime boat ride under a sky full of brilliant stars with the lights of Tortola twinkling in the distance is hard to beat!

Ferries run back and forth to Tortola from Jost Van Dyke, Virgin Gorda (North Sound and the Valley), Cooper Island, Peter Island, and Marina Cay, and also St. Thomas and St. John in the U.S. Virgin Islands. Ferries run from the Valley on Virgin Gorda to St. Thomas (USVI). Ferries also run between Jost Van Dyke and St. Thomas and St. John on weekends.

Two ferry lines run between both Tortola and the Valley on Virgin Gorda and Tortola and St. Thomas. When you arrive at the dock, representatives from each company may try to convince you to take their ferry. Although the people are well-meaning, it can be annoying and confusing when you are trying to pay the cab driver and don't know which ferry you want. If you haven't already decided what ferry to take, just say so firmly and you will be left alone.

FERRY ROUTES AROUND THE BVI

SEE PAGES 138-140 FOR FERRY SCHEDULES

"Ferries are an extremely pleasant way to travel around the BVI."

AMAZING NIGHTS
IN THE BVI

★ Anchoring in Cane Garden Bay and hearing
the melodic sounds of local recording star
Quito Rhymer
drift across the water—beautiful ballads
and love songs accompanied by sweet guitar

★ Any beach on a moonless night,
when the sky is ablaze with about 10 times more stars
than you have ever before seen

★ Bomba's Full-Moon Parties on Tortola,
when there seem to be more people
than you thought lived in the entire BVI

★ Foxy's much-loved and very famous
New Year's Eve extravaganzas
on Jost Van Dyke—when there are
so many boats at anchor
that you can practically hop
from boat to boat all the way to the shore

★ Dancing cheek-to-cheek under the stars
at elegant Biras Creek or Little Dix Bay

★ Walking a deserted beach
under a brilliant full moon, when it's so bright
that the possibility of "moon-burn"
occurs to you for the very first time

7. MARINA CAY

to Scrub I.

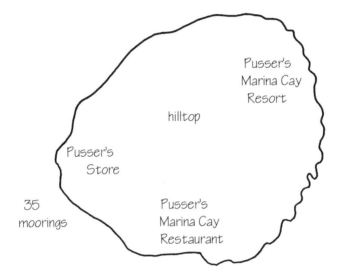

Pusser's
Marina Cay
Resort

hilltop

Pusser's
Store

35
moorings

Pusser's
Marina Cay
Restaurant

to the Beef I.
Ferry Dock
⇩

↑
N

MARINA CAY

This tiny bit of rock that pokes its head out of the water between Beef Island and Great Camanoe is hardly big enough to be called an island. Indeed, it covers just eight acres! It's a great anchorage and there are 35 moorings here and it's the site of the Pusser's Marina Cay Resort, Pusser's Marina Cay Restaurant, and a Pusser's Company Store.

WHAT YOU CAN DO ON MARINA CAY

You can dine or have a drink at the restaurant and shop in Pusser's. You can also sun yourself on the little beach, swim in calm water, and enjoy great snorkeling over the shallow reef that extends out from much of this islet. It's possible to walk completely around Marina Cay in a relatively short amount of time provided you have shoes to protect your feet from the rocks and the sharp coral. There's a second little beach past the docks and a bunch of rocks.

HOW TO GET THERE

There are free ferries from Beef Island at the ferry dock on Trellis Bay. (*See page 140 for schedules.*)

Pusser's Marina Cay Restaurant (*494.2174*) sits along the edge of the beach and is open for lunch and dinner (and breakfast for hotel guests). Appetizers include conch fritters and Caribbean nachos. At lunch you can get hot dogs, burgers, burritos, and various salads. The dinner menu includes ribs, steak, lobster, fish, and pasta. *LD $$*

Pusser's Company Store (*494.2174*) is built out over the water and features the Pusser's line of wearable clothing for the whole family, plus books, nautical memorabilia, swimwear, postcards, and much more.

Pusser's Marina Cay Resort units are on the opposite side of the hillside from the restaurant and look out over the water. Four rooms each have a king size bed, a little refrigerator, ceiling fans (no air-conditioning, but it's almost always very breezy here), and balcony. There are also two two-bedroom suites. Continental breakfast is included in the rates. Guests can rent hobie cats or ocean kayaks or head across to Trellis Bay to windsurf. And, of course, they can take the ferry to Beef Island and explore Tortola for the day. *6 units. Rates: $195 a night for two ($135 off-season); suites $450 ($295 off-season). General Managers: Roger and Sandy Garside. Tel: 284.494.2174. Fax: 284.494.4775. P.O. Box 626. Web: www.pussers.com*

ANGUILLA FOR THE DAY

You're already in the Caribbean. Why not have a great adventure and go downisland for the day?

Anguilla is just 87 miles to the east of Virgin Gorda. It's the "next" island down in the leeward chain. Anguilla is a flat island with gorgeous beaches, great restaurants, and some very fancy hotels, but it's also a quiet and immensely friendly island. (Be sure to bring your passport.)

The Flight.
The 10-seater leaves from the Virgin Gorda airstrip at 9:15 am and departs from the Anguilla airport at 3:15 pm. (Sometimes you can be picked up at and returned to the Tortola/Beef Island airport.) You'll fly over Sombrero, a little island almost no one has ever heard of, that lies halfway between Virgin Gorda and Anguilla. On the way back, the pilot will fly you over the Baths for a great bird's-eye view of these giant boulders and stunning blue water.

On Anguilla.
A tour guide meets you and takes you on a tour around Anguilla, stopping by the well-known Cap Juluca Hotel, the Malliouhana Hotel, and beautiful beaches, and then to Shoal Bay for a light lunch. If you are all one group and want to alter the tour, just ask when you make reservations.

The Details.
The plane is a 10-seater, the flight is 40 minutes, and the fee (including lunch) is $250 per person for 4 or 5 people, and slightly less per person for 6-9 people. (A couple can go by themselves, but the minimum price is $900.) Call 284.495.5346 and ask for Derick Gumbs or call the Anguilla office at 264.497.8690 or fax 264.497.8689 or e-mail transang@anguillanet.com

CHARTERING A SAILBOAT

The British Virgin Islands are one of the most popular chartering areas in the world. If you have ever dreamed about a boating vacation, this is the place to come. You can be your own captain, or hire one.

The BVI nautical environment is almost perfect for charterers. The trade winds blow steadily and the waters are relatively calm. There are a zillion wonderful anchorages, many off of deserted islands. There are also many, many anchorages with moorings, so you can just sail in and pick one up, rather than worry all night about whether your anchor is dragging. In addition, because the islands are so close together, line of sight navigation is almost always possible and, if it gets a bit too windy or rough wherever you are, there is almost always a nearby bay to slip into for shelter.

Because the BVI is so popular with charterers, there are many islands with beach bars just awaiting your arrival. You won't want to miss stopping at the Cooper Island Beach Club, Norman Island (where you'll find great snorkeling and a beach bar and restaurant and the famous Willy T's), Cane Garden Bay, and, of course, famous Foxy's on Jost Van Dyke.

The Moorings is the world's largest chartering operation and they have a huge fleet at their Road Town base. Catamarans and 51' yachts are the most popular and you can bareboat or go with a captain. (*Tel: 888.952.8420, 284.494.2331. Web: www.moorings.com*). Another reliable outfit is Barecat Charters at Soper's Hole. They specialize in catamarans, which many prefer to charter because of comfort and stability. (*Tel: 800.296.5287, 284.495.1979. Web: www.barecat.com*).

8. NECKER

Necker I.

Devil Hill

Devil Hill Bay

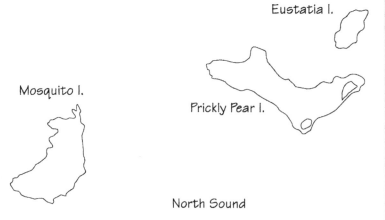

Eustatia I.

Mosquito I.

Prickly Pear I.

North Sound

Virgin Gorda

⇧ N

NECKER

Necker is a luxurious, 74-acre private island surrounded by coral reefs that sits just north of Virgin Gorda and you rent the whole thing. This is the place to come if you want a lot of privacy and plenty of pampering. Mel Gibson, Harrison Ford, Oprah Winfrey, and Steven Spielberg are just some of the many famous guests who have rented here. You can swim at empty beaches, dine on gourmet food, and walk along winding paths through brilliant tropical flowers. At stops on every walk are baskets full of sodas, wine, and cold champagne, just in case that's what you were thinking of having.

For two separate weeks during the year, one can experience Necker without reserving the entire island. During these Celebration Weeks, up to 13 couples (who probably don't know each other) arrive to a kind of "house-party" setting, with their own private bedroom and bath, but sharing the living quarters and dining together.

Necker Island is a truly luxurious tropical paradise. White sand beaches ring the shoreline and brilliant tropical flowers seem to be everywhere. Perched on a hill is a Balinese villa with a sort of giant, high-ceilinged, indoor-outdoor living room open to soft breezes. Bedroom doors fold back completely, providing awesome views right from your pillow. Three Balinese villas have additional bedrooms. Resident chefs work magic in the state-of-the-art kitchen and a staff of 24 await your requests. Paths lead through the manicured grounds to beaches, swimming pools, tennis court, a 300-year old Hindu meditation hut, and hidden hammocks. *General Managers: Rebecca Leigh and Martijn Brower. Daily rates: $22,500 1-14 people, $28,500 15-20 people, $36,000 21-26 people. Celebration Weeks: $19,500 per couple for the week. Rates include almost everything. Reservations: 800.557.4255. Web: www.neckerisland.com*

SEAGRAPE COTTAGE ON LITTLE THATCH

If you want something a bit smaller than Necker, head to this breezy West Indian beachfront cottage with kitchen on a 55-acre private island just west of Tortola and perfect for honeymooners. The island's owners visit their hilltop villa but much of the time the island will feel like it's all yours. Rent a boat to explore other islands. *General Managers: Jon and Katy Morley. Weekly rates for two people: $6,500 ($5,000 off-season) plus provisioning, if requested. Tel: 284.495.9227. Fax: 284.495.9212. Web: www.littlethatchisland.com*

RAINY DAYS

*Rainy days are rare in the British Virgin Islands but if it
happens to rain on one of the days you are in the BVI, here
are some great things to do.*

❖Schedule a massage or a yoga class
at Fort Recovery.

❖Find someone you love and take a
long rainy walk on the beach.

❖Get a book and read quietly where you can
see and hear the rain and
smell the tropical moisture
but still keep dry
(in light rains a palm tree is fine shelter).

❖Write and send a dozen postcards to people you
like, or to people you don't like.

❖Go for a swim in a pool.

❖Play a board game, like Parcheesi or Clue. Most
places have these games around
and they're still fun, whether you are 12 or 112.

❖Take photographs—rain showers, rainbows, slick
palm fronds, patterns of rain on water.

❖Sit, listen, and watch...spend time just pausing.

SCUBA DIVING

Many people have no idea that dive outfits in the BVI offer simple Resort Courses where qualified instructors teach you how to dive in just a few hours, in the safety of a quiet pool, and then take you out for a real dive over a reef or a wreck. You go down 40 to 50 feet with trained instructors by your side.

Many who have tried this go on to become certified divers. Almost everybody says that it is an amazing and wonderful experience, and some say it is even easier than snorkeling.

For experienced divers, the BVI offer some exceptionally interesting shipwrecks, including the 2,434 ton *H.M.S. Rhone*, plus caves, reefs, walls, pinnacles, ledges, and archways, all in unusually clear water. Night dives, which show off amazing things you can't see underwater during the day, are popular here, too.

*On Tortola, call **Blue Water Divers** at Nanny Cay and Soper's Hole (494.2847) (495.1200) or **Underwater Safaris** at The Moorings in Road Town (494.3235).*

*On Virgin Gorda **DIVE BVI** works out of Leverick Bay (495.7328) and the Virgin Gorda Yacht Harbour (495.5513) and also at Marina Cay. **Kilbride's Underwater Tours** is at the Bitter End Yacht Club on Virgin Gorda's North Sound (495.9638).*

9. PETER

Sprat Bay

Great Harbour

Deadman's Bay

Reef Bay

Great Snorkeling

White Bay

Five-Mile Walk

Carrot Rock

N

PETER

Peter Island is a lush and mountainous private island five miles south of Tortola. The Peter Island Resort and Yacht Harbour is nestled along the north shore and there are five beautiful beaches. What magazine articles and books omit about this resort is that the resort facilities only take up a tiny bit of this four-and-a-half-mile-long island. The rest of the island is undeveloped, except for the Eagle's Nest, a private residence that sits atop the island's highest point. Although there are no cars on the island, several roads lead through this hilly woodland and there are marvelous opportunities for long, scenic walks, including the famous five-mile walk that starts from Sprat Bay. Several bays on Peter Island are popular anchorages and there are moorings on Sprat Bay. The ferry schedule (see page 140) makes it easy to come from Road Town for lunch or dinner.

Peter Island Resort and Yacht Harbour has just 52 rooms, 32 on a spit of land looking out over the Sir Francis Drake Channel, and another 20 clustered at one end of Deadman's Bay. The Beach rooms, located on a low bluff at the western edge of Deadman's Bay, are spacious, with romantic bathtubs that open onto tropical greenery. There are four to a building, two upstairs and two downstairs. The lower units open onto grassy areas and stairs that lead to the beach and the upper units have higher ceilings, a bit more privacy, and more dramatic views. The rooms near the dock are smaller and are also four to a building. The first floor Garden View rooms look out across the pool or into the gardens and have a little sitting alcove. The slightly smaller second-floor Ocean View rooms with high ceilings look across the pool and gardens to the water. There are five beaches, a water sports program, a disappearing-edge swimming pool, tennis courts, a fitness trail, and an exercise room.

The Tradewinds Restaurant is the resort's signature restaurant and it is air-conditioned but can be opened to the island breezes. Breakfast is served here daily. Dinner is a la carte and there is a different, and extensive, menu every night but Saturday, when there is a Grand Buffet. Deadman's Bay Bar and Grill is open every day for lunch and offers both a buffet and an a la carte menu. Dinner is served here several nights a week. Both restaurants are expensive.

52 units, 3 private villas. Rates including all meals: $840-$990 ($530-$680 off-season) plus 17% tax and service charge. Managing Director: Wayne Kafcsak. Reservations: 800.346.4451. Tel: 284.495.2000. Fax: 284.495.2500. P.O. Box 211. Web: www.peterisland.com

ONE PERFECT DAY IN PARADISE

✻ An early wake up and a walk to watch the
sun rise out of the Caribbean sea

✻ A read and a rest until breakfast

✻ Some swimming, sunning, sailing or
snorkeling

✻ A light lunch by the water's edge

✻ A rest in your room

✻ Some biking or hiking or just
exploring the sights

✻ A warm shower and change

✻ A cool drink as the sun slips into the ocean

✻ Dinner, a dance, a dip in the pool

✻ A stargazing trip to the beach

✻ And back to the room for sweet dreams

GREAT THINGS TO DO

Float - just lie on one of those wonderful floats in the warm Caribbean and do nothing, just float.

Walk on a beach at night - take in the sounds and sights, the stars, the moon, and look for the magic of the sparkling phosphorescence at the water's edge.

Experience a sunrise along a beach - you don't have to do it the morning after your night beach walk, and you don't have to stay up all night. Just get up a little early (you can always go back to bed).

Do a Drive - pick one of the drives in this book or make one up, but do get up in the hills of Tortola or Virgin Gorda for some magnificent views.

Go somewhere in a boat - go anywhere or nowhere.

Spend an hour alone doing nothing - inside or out, day or night - no TV, no tapes, no writing, no reading, just you and yourself for an hour doing absolutely nothing.

Catch the BBC news from London - it's on radio ZBVI.

Take a day trip to another island - go to Jost or Anegada or Tortola or an uninhabited cay.

Go to a horse race - they're held once a month at the track at Sea Cow's Bay, and they're a lot of fun!

See the islands from the air - If you missed this because you arrived by ferry, then call Fly BVI so you won't miss the spectacular views from a plane!

10. TORTOLA

Long Bay (West)

BEEF ISLAND

Elizabeth Bay
Lambert Bay

Maya Cove

Josiah's Bay

Brandywine Bay

Skyworld

Road Town & Harbour

Brewer's Bay

Cane Garden
Bay

Nanny Cay

Apple Bay

Long Bay (East)

Smuggler's
Cove

Frenchman's Cay

Soper's Hole

⇐ N

TORTOLA IN A NUTSHELL

Tortola is the largest British Virgin Island and exceptionally hilly. There is virtually no flat land. Houses are scattered on the steep hillsides and roads hug the shoreline or run feverishly up and down the island's multiple peaks showing off stunning, airplane-like views.

This island is by far the most populated British Virgin Island, with over 17,000 people (or over 80% of the entire BVI population). Nestled against Tortola's south shore is Road Town, the capital of the BVI.

Road Town, which is built almost entirely on reclaimed land, is the only real "town" in the entire country. Government buildings, plus grocery, plumbing, office supply, and hardware stores are mixed in with the bars, restaurants, shops, and marinas that are fun to visit. There's also a cruise ship dock, public ferry dock, and Customs Office.

At the west end of the island is West End, where there is a public ferry dock and Customs Office, plus a marina, some shops, and a Pusser's Restaurant and Store. The east end of the island, including Beef Island (which is only 600 feet from Tortola and the location of the airport), is less developed but has some excellent restaurants and art galleries.

The best beaches, some with little restaurants and bars, some completely undeveloped, are strung along Tortola's entire north shore.

WHAT YOU CAN DO ON TORTOLA

Swim, snorkel, hike, horseback ride, see stunning views, walk along exceptionally beautiful beaches, drive remarkably hilly roads, eat outside almost all the time day and night—whether you're at a local "fish fry" or a fancy gourmet restaurant, drink barefoot at beachside bars, rent a boat, take a boat ride . . . the list goes on and on. Shopping is on a small scale but there are great things to buy if you know where on the island to look.

GETTING TO TORTOLA FROM NEARBY ISLANDS

Tortola is reachable by ferry from North Sound and The Valley on Virgin Gorda, Peter Island, Jost Van Dyke, and St. Thomas and St. John in the USVI *(See page 135 for routes here from the U.S and UK.)*

EXPLORING TORTOLA

Spectacular panoramic vistas are one of Tortola's most outstanding features. Although the roads are remarkably steep in places, many people will want to rent a car and drive, at least once, to catch these stunning views. If you are truly faint of heart, then opt for a taxi tour.

TORTOLA'S AMAZING ROADS

On Tortola, there's almost no such thing as a straight, flat piece of road. This mountainous island isn't a single steep mound, but rather a collection of many, many knobby hilltops. Tortola's road system is draped over these knobs, dropping swiftly to sea level every once in a while to skirt a shimmering bay or run along a crescent of beach.

The roads themselves are astonishing: a collection of hairpin turns and dizzying descents and ascents that often are bordered by precipitous drops. Because of this, Tortola's scenery is especially spectacular from a car. When you are driving on this island you are constantly changing altitude and frequently looking across plummeting valleys to other hilltops, with sweeping views of the sea and other islands beyond. There are many views from over 1000 feet.

Renting a jeep or a car. In Road Town, delightful Ms. Burke at **ITGO** (*494.2639*) at the Mill Mall complex is the person to see. At West End, **Hertz** (*495.4405*), right next to the Jolly Roger, is a good bet. **Dollar Rent A Car** has offices at Long Bay Resort (*495.4772*) and also at Prospect Reef (*494.6093*) just outside of Road Town. **National** (*494.3197*) has an office at Long Bay Resort. Jeeps run $50-60 a day, somewhat less off-season. You'll need a temporary BVI license ($10 plus a valid license from home), which is easily available through the rental agency. And remember, driving is on the left.

Hiring a taxi and taxi tours. Almost any taxi will take you around part or all of the island for about $45. Mr. Hilroy Douglas (*494.4064, cell 499.3975*) is a good choice for an island tour or if you need to be picked up at a certain time to catch a plane or a ferry. If you need a taxi in West End, call 495.4934 or 495.4881; in Road Town call 494.3456 or 494.6456; in East End call Bob's at 496.7136 or 495.1982. Expect to share taxis with fellow travelers. Fares, which are for two or more people, range from $3 per person for a short ride (such as from one part of Road Town to another) to $12 per person from West End to Road Town to $18 per person from one end of Tortola to the other. Even if you rent a car, it can be more relaxing to take a taxi to a distant restaurant.

HINTS FOR DRIVING ON TORTOLA

❏On steep hills, in automatic cars, if you can't get enough power, even in low gear, turn off the air-conditioning and you'll be okay.

❏Driving is on the left. This is the trickiest when you are turning from one road onto another or heading into a round-a-bout. Invent a reminder, like staying on the same side of the road as your heart.

❏Share the driving. Managing the roads requires constant attention, so the driver misses the views.

❏Try to keep track, on a map, of where you think you are so you'll recognize a turn. There are few road signs and the twists and turns happen fast.

❏Hills and curves look completely different from the other direction, so a road you have just driven can look totally unfamiliar on the return trip. Don't feel stupid. You're not lost.

❏Beware those tight little curves you see on a map—those are hills! However, distances are short, and almost everything is only 10 minutes away from the last thing, even if it is over switchbacks.

❏Tailgaters are common, and can hang unnervingly close behind you. If they annoy you, pull to the side and let them pass. When you tire of doing this, just stop looking in the rearview mirror.

❏Speaking of mirrors, keep a lookout for mirrors on hills and curves. These are specially positioned to give you a view of oncoming traffic that you can't otherwise see.

❏When you encounter goats or cows being herded along the road, just slow down and politely make your way through. Watch also for the stray goat, or cow, or horse that is standing in the road intently munching on the leaves of an overhanging tree branch.

❏Do be very careful. "Island time" doesn't seem to apply to driving here and you'll encounter Indianapolis 500 wanna-bes.

A SPECTACULAR
TEN-MINUTE DRIVE

FROM ROAD TOWN TO SKYWORLD

This drive takes you on an ear-popping 1300 foot ascent in about eight breathtaking minutes. It's an awesome trip in both directions. At the top is an observation deck with the highest 360 degree view in the BVI. It's possible to see Anegada and even St. Croix which is 40 miles away. There's also a great restaurant, Skyworld, and a neat little shop.

Time: 10 minutes each way, plus however long you stay mesmerized by the view at Skyworld.
When to do this: On clear days you can see the farthest. Sunsets here are gorgeous.

From Pusser's in Road Town, head east from the waterfront (the water is on your right) toward the center of Road Town. Stay on this road several minutes, until you come to a round-a-bout. Bear left, into the round-a-bout, and take your very first left out of the round-a-bout, by the Shell station. You'll come to a "T" in the road. Turn right onto Main Street (keeping, of course, to the left side of the road). Take your first real left, which will head uphill. Sometimes this road sign says Joe's Hill Road, sometimes it says Cane Garden Bay, and sometimes it's not there. Soon after you've turned, those on the right side of the car can start looking down at some great views of Road Town and Road Harbour.

After some sharp twists back and forth, there is an extremely severe switchback curve that climbs up at an almost impossible angle. (Your ears should have popped by now.) The switchback spits you out onto an almost level bit of road. Bear right after you pass a white two-story building on your left.

Soon you'll see a spectacular view of neighboring islands on the left. There are several little pull-off areas on your left where you can stop to look at the views and take photographs.

Watch for the sign to Skyworld. It's on the left but the turn is actually to the right, and it's an extremely sharp right turn that also heads up.

67

After you turn right, you'll pass an elementary school (imagine going to school every day and having these views out your window!) and then you'll be on a narrow ridge with a pasture sweeping down to your left. Just ahead is a hill.

Now is the time to look for the entrance to Skyworld. The sign isn't always there but it's your first left and it is steep. Drive straight up until you are spilled out onto a little plateau with a parking lot. Pull in, get out, and enjoy the view.

From here, looking south, you can see the entire chain of islands that border the Sir Francis Drake Channel. From left to right, they are the south end of Virgin Gorda, Fallen Jerusalem, Round Rock (the little one), Ginger, Cooper, Salt, Peter, Norman, and tiny Pelican Island. The small island farthest to the right is the easternmost USVI which is called Flanagan Island.

For a lunch or beverage with a great view, head to the entrance of the building, which is the Skyworld Restaurant. To reach the observation deck, follow the path just to the right of the restaurant entrance, which leads around to a set of stairs. There is a gift shop there, too.

RETURNING FROM SKYWORLD
Retracing your steps is easy except for one place. After you've turned right out of the Skyworld driveway, and turned left after the school, you'll be on level road for a while. Watch for the white two-story house and take the abrupt left just before the house. Be prepared for some truly spectacular airplane-like views as you drop about 1100 feet in the four or five minutes it takes to get back to sea level. To get back to the round-a-bout when you reach the bottom of this amazing hill, go left and then take your first right. Follow it to the end, turn left, and you'll be back in the round-a-bout.

> "Be prepared for some truly spectacular
> airplane-like views as you drop about 1100 feet
> in the four or five minutes it takes
> to get back to sea level."

TORTOLA'S GREAT BEACHES

Tortola's best beaches are tucked along the island's north shore. It's here that you will find picture-perfect crescents of glistening white sand bordered by sea grapes and palm trees. Some are very easy to reach. Others have bumpy and steep approaches. You may be the only one on the beach and there are no lifeguards so be careful when swimming.

Apple Bay, home of the famous Bomba's Shack, is a narrow strip of beach that is the most popular surfing beach because of the rollers coming in from the Atlantic.

Brewer's Bay is a long and bumpy ride down but worth the discomfort. It's a calm beach great for swimming and snorkeling. The access from Ridge Road, just east of the Cool Breeze Bar, is the easiest approach. A restaurant and bar is at the west end of the beach.

Cane Garden Bay is the closest beach to Road Town (just 15 minutes) even though it's on the north shore. Because it is so accessible and so famous, it can just be too crowded some days on season. Definitely skip it when cruise ships are in Road Town. It's too picturesque to miss completely, so try stopping by in the early morning or evening or anytime off-season. To get there from Road Town, just follow the directions to Skyworld (page 67) but go straight instead of right when you see the first Skyworld sign and follow the road down to sea level.

Lambert Beach is on the eastern end of Tortola's north shore. It's usually a good swimming beach unless the surf is up and then watch out for strong undertows. Lambert Beach Resort is here, and you can use their immense pool for a small fee.

Josiah's Bay Beach is often completely deserted. Some days this east end beach can have strong undertows. Follow Little Dick's Road from the Long Look Police Station and go right at the sign (before the hill).

Long Bay Beach (East) is actually on Beef Island and is long and lovely and good for swimming. Head toward the airport but turn left just past the salt flats and then follow the dirt road which curves to the right around the flats (and please don't drive across the flats).

Long Bay Beach (West) is a stunning mile-long stretch of white sand that is never crowded. Tortola's best resort, Long Bay Beach Resort, fronts part of it and has a nice beach restaurant and bar. Nathan's Place (no sign), run by Chef Myra, is a delightful casual spot for lunch at the western end of the beach (*see page 86*).

Smuggler's Cove takes a bit of bouncing around to get to but it's one of Tortola's most picture-perfect beaches. A wide crescent of white sand wraps along most of the shore and the water is the color of turquoise neon light. This bay is almost always calm and on some days can be as still as a pond. The bottom is sandy and deepens very gradually. *(See page 77 for a more complete description.)*

70

THINGS THAT ARE FUN TO DO ON TORTOLA

❏Go to the airport and watch little planes land and take off. The Beef Island airport has a great observation deck.

❏Visit the Botanic Gardens in Road Town (across from the Police Station). They're open daily from 8 am to 6 pm and you'll see all kinds of flowers and plants and a special section on medicinal plants.

❏Go to a local sporting event. Check the local papers or stop by the Tourist Board in Road Town to see what is going on. There can be softball games, rugby matches, horse races, and sailing regattas.

❏Head to the docks and watch the boats come and go. You'll see vessels of all sizes, both power and sail. It's fun to watch the skilled skippers navigate so effortlessly, and even more fun to watch some of the less-experienced charterers try to manage. In Road Town, go to Village Cay Marina or the Moorings . At West End, go to Pusser's on Frenchman's Cay.

❏Drive or take a taxi to the observation platform at Skyworld. It is less than 10 minutes from Road Town and the views are unmatchable. Bring your camera and just keep shooting. This is the highest unobstructed 360 degree view in the BVI.

❏Go horseback riding. Shadow (*494.2262*) offers great guided riding trips up into the hills and down along the beaches.

GREAT WATER SPORTS

Cane Garden Bay on Tortola and Trellis Bay on Beef Island are two very protected bays and are the two most popular areas for windsurfing, kayaking, and sunfishing. You can also go water-skiing on Cane Garden Bay. On calm days it is wonderful fun to rent your own little powerboat and go wherever you want.

WINDSURFING, WATER-SKIING, AND KAYAKING

Cane Garden Bay Pleasure Boats (*495.9660*) rents Hobie Cats, sailboats, sunfish, windsurfers, kayaks, canoes, and snorkel equipment. Prices range from $15 an hour for a sunfish to $25 an hour for a Hobie Cat. You can go water-skiing for about $50 a half hour or $75 an hour.

Boardsailing BVI (*495.2447*) at Trellis Bay on Beef Island rents equipment by the hour, day, and week, and offers all levels of instruction.

RENTING LITTLE POWERBOATS

Cane Garden Bay Pleasure Boats (*495.9660*) rents 18'-24' powerboats with a bimini, cooler, and ship-to-shore radio for $200-$350 a day, including fuel.

M & M Powerboat Rentals (*495.9993*), at Village Cay, rents 22' 150 hp powerboats with a bimini for $250 a day, plus fuel.

Sheppard Powerboat Rentals (*495.4099*) operates out of his own marina at Soper's Hole and rents Mako 25' power boats with a center console and bimini for $275 per day plus fuel. A captain is $100 additional per day.

HAVE LUNCH OR DINNER
ON ANOTHER ISLAND!

If you are staying on Tortola and want to have dinner on Virgin Gorda (or visa versa), call **Speedy's** (*495.5235, 495.5240*), which has a ferry leaving for Virgin Gorda at 6:45 pm and returning at 10:30 pm and leaving Virgin Gorda at 6 pm and returning at 11 pm. (*See page 138 for daytime schedules.*) If you want to go to Cooper or Jost Van Dyke or any other island for dinner (or for the day), or if you just need transportation to another island and want to take a water taxi, then call **Sheppard Power Boat Rentals and Water Taxis** (*495.4099*).

GREAT SNORKEL TRIPS AND BOAT TRIPS TO OTHER ISLANDS

Remarkably, from Tortola, it's only three to five miles to all the other British Virgin Islands, except far-flung Anegada, and there are excellent boat trips available to all the islands, even Anegada. For a very reasonable price you can go with a group or charter a small boat with a captain. These trips leave from Road Town or Soper's Hole at West End. Almost all take all major credit cards.

Most boat trips head to other islands and to several great snorkeling spots. Exactly where they go will depend on the weather that day, and especially on how windy it is. Some of these trips stop at a restaurant on an island and others serve lunch on board.

If you know how to handle boats and prefer to be in charge, you can also rent a little powerboat and take yourself on your own snorkel trip. It's best to do this when the weather is calm. Call Sheppard at Sheppard Powerboat Rentals (495.4099) or Ash Harrigan at Power Boat Rentals, Ltd. (495.5542).

What to bring? Towel and bathing suit, sunscreen, your own snorkel gear if you have a prescription mask, camera, and film.

Aristocat Charters (*499.1249, 495.4087, www.aristocatcharters.com*) offers half-day, full-day, and sunset cruises on a spacious, stable 48' catamaran. Lunch, beverages, and snorkel gear are provided. The boat sails from Soper's Hole in West End and destinations can include Jost Van Dyke, Norman, and Peter Islands. Rates are $90 per person for a full day, maximum 14 people.

Black Angel Cruises (*495.3483, 499.1437, www.blackangelcruises.com*) specializes in taking two to six people on tailor-made day trips (or two people on splendid overnight—or longer—adventures). They can suggest an itinerary or go where you decide. Try an afternoon snorkel and a sunset or perhaps a full day of snorkeling and visiting deserted beaches or perhaps just a glorious sail, some of the time with your hand at the wheel. The spacious and shaded cockpit comfortably seats six and there is deck space for sunning. Based at Nanny Cay, the Black Angel is a 45' sloop with a sleek black hull. Rates are $150 per person for a full day (including lunch) and $800 for two people for two nights (including gourmet meals).

73

High Seas Adventures (*495.1300, www.highseabvi.com*) takes people on half-and full day snorkeling trips all over the BVI on a 28' boat. Pickups are at Penn's Landing and Village Cay. Captain Roy has been doing this for years and he's incredibly knowledgeable, known for his teaching abilities, and happy to teach kids of all ages. Half-day trips might go to the Indians and Norman, or Salt Island and the Wreck of the Rhone plus Cooper and are from 9:30 am to1 pm and 1 pm to 5 pm. Full days (9:30 am to 5 pm and 3 snorkeling stops) can be your choice of The Baths, on to North Sound, and then snorkeling at one of the Dogs, or to Jost Van Dyke via Sandy Cay and Green Cay. Half days are $60 a person. Full days are $80 a person, including refreshments.

Goddess Athena (*494.0000, www.virginathena.com*), an 84' ketch, is known as the "little pirate ship" and is one of the most famous charter boats in the Caribbean. This spacious luxury vessel specializes in elegant day-sail "excursion cruises" to islands around Tortola. Appealing day trips range from a Jost Van Dyke Lobster Feast to Snorkeling at Cooper Island to Around Tortola in a Day. They also do evening champagne cruises and seasonal "theme" cruises. Prices range from $45 to $120 per person.

Patouche Charters (*494.6300, www.patouche.com*) offers snorkeling trips to nearby islands via catamaran and includes guided underwater tours and snorkel instruction. These are good trips for people who have never snorkeled, but seasoned snorkelers will also enjoy it because of the destinations. Choose between a half day and one ot two snorkel stops or a full day and two or three snorkel stops plus lunch. In either case, you'll be with 6 to 16 other people. They usually go snorkeling near Norman, Cooper, and Peter. Rates per person are $60 half day (one-two snorkel sites) and $100 for a full day (two-three snorkel sites and lunch). They have several boats, including the Sandy Cay, a Bertram that used to be part of the Little Dix fleet. Private charters are available on any of their boats and they will customize a trip just for you!

Silmaril (*495.9225, www.charteraboat.com/silmaril*) is a 41' sailing yacht based at Peter Island. Paul and Judy will come pick you up anywhere on the south side of Tortola for a day (or half day) of whatever you want to do. They are happy to let you tailor the trip but they'll make suggestions or plan it for you if you wish. You can decide whether you want to eat on board or at a beach bar or gourmet restaurant and whether you want to spend more time sailing or resting at anchor or snorkeling. The rate is $450 per day for one to four people. Half days (morning, afternoon, or into sunset) are $320 for one to four people. Overnight charters are $750 per night (two night minimum) including your beverages.

Speedy's Ferry Service (*495.5240*) offers a day trip to Virgin Gorda from Road Town which includes transportation to The Baths and lunch at the Bath & Turtle Restaurant. No advance reservation is needed. Just be there before 9 am and be sure the boat you get on is Speedy's, not Smith's. The boat leaves at 9 am from the public ferry dock in Road Town and leaves Virgin Gorda for the trip back at 3:30 pm (4 pm Sunday). Cost is $25 a person ($15 for children).

White Squall II (*494.2564, www.whitesquall2.com*) heads to the Baths on Virgin Gorda and Cooper Island or goes to Norman Island and the Indians. It's a traditional 80' schooner so there may be a lot of people but there is still plenty of room. Rates include a barbecue lunch with wine, rum punch, and beer, and complimentary snorkel equipment. The boat sails at 9:30 am from Village Cay Marina in Road Town. Rates are $85 per person.

Kuralu (*495.4381, www.kuralu.com*) is a 50' luxury cruising catamaran that is so popular it's booked almost every day. Robin Pinfold is the owner and captain, and his charming golden retriever is often first mate! This is a fine trip for families and children as there is safety netting around the boat. Choose from two trips. One goes to Green Cay for snorkeling and then makes a great spinnaker sail to Jost Van Dyke. After lunch on board, you can swim or snorkel and stop at Foxy's before the return sail. The other trip goes to the Indians for snorkeling and to Benures Bay where you can swim with big turtles. Lunch is usually several salads, quiche, a variety of cheeses and cold meats, and French bread. Since Robin is usually out every day, just leave a message on his machine saying where and when you want to go, the number of people, and where you are staying. He'll be sure to get back to you that evening. Trips are around $90 per person (around $45 for children under 12).

Remember, the Caribbean sun is stronger than up north—wear a hat and lots of sun block on your nautical adventure! And don't forget your camera.

SPAS, SPORTS, AND FITNESS ON TORTOLA

HIKING

Trails to Sage Mountain National Park show off a great view from the highest point on Tortola, 1780'. You can also hike from Brewer's Bay to Mount Healthy National Park where there is a restored 18th-century windmill. It's a great place for a picnic.

HORSEBACK RIDING

Shadow has very gentle horses and will take two to six people on guided rides to Brewer's Bay, Cane Garden Bay, and along Ridge Road. Instruction is also available. Call Shadow at **Shadow's Stables** (*494.2262*) on Ridge Road just east of Skyworld. Do wear long pants.

TENNIS

You'll find six courts at **Prospect Reef Resort** (*495.3311*) and three courts at the **Long Bay Beach Resort** (*495.4252*) and non-hotel guests are welcome at both for a nominal charge.

SPAS AND THERAPEUTIC MASSAGE

When you want to cool down and be pampered, you'll find some soothing spas on Tortola. Be sure to call ahead for appointments.

The **Golden Palms Wellness Spa** (*495.4252 or 494.0138*) at Long Bay Beach Resort has a full menu of body wraps and offers therapeutic massage, facials, manicures, and saunas. In Road Town, the **Oasis** (*494.8891*) can take care of everything from hair color to foil highlights to acrylic nails and body wraps.

The inviting **Almond Tree Salon & Day Spa** (*495.4208*) at Nanny Cay (halfway between West End and Road Town) is the place to go for a great haircut (men or women) or haircolor. It's the winner of the Best Hair Stylist and Best Hair Colorist in both the USVI and BVI.

At **Fort Recovery** (*495.4467*), Pamelah Jacobson specializes in a combination of Swedish, Shiatsu, and Reflexology massage.

YOGA CLASSES

Yoga classes are given by appointment (24-hour notice please) at **Fort Recovery** (*495.4467*).

A "SMUGGLER'S" ADVENTURE

Smuggler's Cove is an out-of-the-way, beautiful beach with good snorkeling and calm water for swimming. It's on the northwest shore of Tortola about eight bumpy minutes from the Long Bay Beach Resort.

This is one of Tortola's most beautiful and most protected beaches. There is a good snorkeling reef which you can easily spot from land. The best snorkeling is out from the shore a bit, just before the little waves are breaking. Those who have been here before will be sad to learn that "Uncle Bob," who ran the Caribbean's most unusual little snack bar, complete with a Lincoln Continental, passed away in 2002.

Directions: Get yourself to Long Bay Beach Resort. The road from here to Smuggler's is almost all dirt but passable (although not necessarily comfortable because of the bumps) in a car although a jeep-type vehicle with a lot of clearance is preferable, especially if it is muddy. The drive only takes about eight minutes but it will seem longer the first time.

Follow the road past Long Bay Beach Resort. Eventually the road veers abruptly left. Start driving up the hill but look for the very first right. It's hard to spot and the turn is abrupt and drops sharply down. However, it's just before the sign for Belmont Estates. (This is one of the most exclusive areas of Tortola and there are many luxurious homes and villas tucked up in these hills.) Take this right, which spills quickly down. Be patient and go slowly. The road ahead is dirt, deeply rutted, and has giant potholes and rocks that can blow a tire, so you have to kind of pick your way around obstacles.

This road winds through tangles of second-growth forest and is woodsy and shady. (You're driving inland a bit to get around a large salt pond.) When the road finally bears right, you'll be in the parking area for Smuggler's Cove. You may see a few other cars, but if you are lucky, you could be the only one. Park along either side of the road.

Returning is a little difficult because there are several turns that lead to nowhere but that look seductively "right." Just keep bearing left whenever you have a choice and eventually you will be back on the road that leads past Long Bay. (When you come to the sign that points right to "Long Bay"you can go right or left. Both roads lead to the road back to Long Bay).

Note: Bring sunscreen, drinking water, and snorkeling gear. Sometimes there is a little snack bar set up to the right of the entrance, but sometimes there isn't.

77

TORTOLA'S TOWNS

If you look at Tortola's curvy shoreline from a plane, you'll see that it is defined by one bay after another. These bays have become Tortola's "landmarks" and the names of Tortola's settlements. People live in Sea Cows Bay, or Carrot Bay, or Baughers Bay, or Soper's Hole. The bays are used to indicate location and you will encounter bay names far more frequently than road names when you ask for directions.

The only big town is Road Town. West End (also referred to as Soper's Hole or Frenchman's Cay), and East End are very tiny towns.

GREAT SHOPPING IN ROAD TOWN

There are many wonderful places to shop in Road Town but they are scattered about (although within easy walking distance from each other). Bear in mind that this is the capital of a country and also by far the country's biggest town. Islanders come here from all over Tortola and from all of the other British Virgin Islands for almost everything they need—from hammers to scotch tape to drivers' licenses. It can be extremely trafficky during weekdays.

Road Town has no separate "tourist" area with a nice little row of boutiques and eateries. It is a real place, with restaurants, bars, and shops tucked in between hardware stores and government agencies. The islanders dress up when they come to Road Town because it is their "city." It's okay for visitors to be casually dressed but bathing suits or short shorts in town are unacceptable. Also, don't be intimidated by a shabby storefront door. Paint and metal are simply no match for the Caribbean sun, wind, and salt air.

GREAT ROAD TOWN SHOPS

There are two main shopping areas in Road Town: Main Street and Wickham's Cay I. Locals use landmarks for directions so it really helps to know the major ones. In Road Town, when you ask where something is, it's usually near Scotia Bank or the round-a-bout or Bobby's (a supermarket) or Bolo's (next to Bobby's). See the map on page 80 for locations. Bolo's, by the way, is an excellent source for everything from batteries to cosmetics.

Great Main Street Shops

These stores are listed in geographical order, beginning at the Post Office.
Esme's Shop (*494.3961*), across from the Post Office, is the place to come when you start feeling "out of touch" and want U.S. newspapers and magazines.

Kaunda's Kysy Tropix 2 (*494.6737*), carries a huge selection of music CDs. Come here for reggae, rap, rock, hip hop, punk, steel bands, and today's hits.

Samarkand (*494.6415*) handcrafts gold and silver jewelry. Many pieces have an island motif—sand dollars, shells, anchors—and make perfect gifts.

Caribbean Handprints (*494.3717*) features pastel silk-screen fabrics, sold by the yard or fashioned into clothing, beach bags, place mats, and more. Bring home a soft kimono and remember the BVI every morning!

Pusser's Company Store (*494.2467*) is home to attractive, wearable clothing for the whole family, bottles of their famous rum, nautical antiques, island books, postcards, and much, much more! Be sure to check out the upstairs.

Jewellery Box (*494.7278*) showcases gold and silver jewelry and one-of-a-kind pieces fashioned out of shells, wood, and the local sandbox plant.

Latitude 18 (*494.7807*), located at Main Street's major curve, carries colorful sportswear and island wear for the whole family. There are great T-shirts, sunglasses, sundresses, pants, shorts, backpacks, bathing suits, sarongs, and rows and rows of great hats. A branch is located at Soper's Hole.

Sunny Caribbee Herb and Spice Co. (*494.2178*) is the place for wonderful exotic spices, "hangover cures," island books, cookbooks, handmade jewelry, island art, and colorful pottery, including some delightful items from Barbados Earthworks. Anything you buy can be shipped home for you.

Serendipity (*494.5865*) features an eclectic mix of books, cards, miniature books, and assorted unusual and very appealing gift ideas. This a great shop to browse around in. The more you look, the more you see. Many items are tiny and very packable.

Caribbean Fine Arts (*494.4240*), at 160 Main Street (look for the pink doors), displays an extensive array of superb watercolors and prints by local artists. There are also pretty note cards for sale. Sylvia Forbes, the owner, is happy to ship your selection home (so you don't have to lug it around) and she also does a fine job of framing.

Great Shopping on Wickhams Cay I

Books Etcetera (*494.6611*), tucked in the marina side of the Mill Mall complex, features New York Times hardcover bestsellers, current newspapers including the New York Times and Wall Street Journal, U.S. magazines, paperbacks, postcards, and beautiful maps of the islands.

Cantik (*494.7927*) is a bit hidden (walk out past the Ample Hamper towards the Captain's Table) but a delight. Come to this outstanding shop for beautiful handmade greeting cards, CDs of island music, wind chimes, candles, clocks embedded in polished wood, watches, fabric, and furniture. (Walk through the furniture to the back room to see everything.) Look for the perfectly-tuned miniature steel drum. Anything you buy here can be shipped anywhere.

Crafts Alive, a collection of pastel-painted West Indian cottages in a park-like setting overlooking Road Town Harbour, is a good place to come for T-shirts, hats, jewelry, and locally-made hot sauces and craft items. Each cottage has something different to offer. This area can be crowded when cruise ships are in and many cottages close on non-cruise ship days.

Richard's Black Coral Jewelry (*494.4717*), on the marina side of the Mill Mall complex, is a showcase for earrings, bracelets, pendants, and other jewelry items crafted out of black coral scraps washed up by the sea. Look for the outstanding coral sculptures of a crab and of a lobster.

Sea Urchin (*494.4108*), in the old Mill, carries an inexhaustible supply of fashionable sandals, beachwear, resortwear, sundresses, sunglasses, and local books for the whole family. Other branches are on Waterfront Drive (next to Capriccio Di Mare) and at West End.

ROAD TOWN LANDMARKS

Round-a-bout
Bobby's
Bolo's

Chalwell St.

Main Street

Waterfront Drive

Ferry Dock

Scotia Bank
Wickhams Cay I
(Mill Mall Complex)

GREAT SHOPPING IN WEST END

West End refers to the area along the shore of Soper's Hole, a deep anchorage at the West End of Tortola. The Customs Office, public ferry docks, Zelma's Variety, and the Jolly Roger Bar and Restaurant are on one side of the harbour. On the other side (which is actually an island called Frenchman's Cay that is connected to the mainland by a bridge) is a small collection of shops and retaurants.

When you feel like food or a drink, stop at **Pusser's** *for a salad or sandwich or their famous painkiller punch or drop into* **Pices** *for burgers and conch fritters.*

Blue Water Divers (*495.1200*) carries bathing suits that let the sun through so you can tan all over (no tan lines) plus diving and snorkeling gear and island books and postcards.

Culture Classic Boutique (*494.6415*) is a tiny shop full of dresses, sarongs, wind chimes, postcards, and T-shirts.

Caribbean Jewellers (*495.4137*), a branch of Road Town's Samarkand, is a showcase for 14K gold and silver jewelry.

Latitude 18 (*494.7807*) features a delightful collection of colorful Caribbean clothing for the whole family. Come here for bathing suits, backpacks, hats, sarongs, sundresses, T-shirts, sunglasses, and more. A sister shop is on Main Street in Road Town.

Pusser's Company Store (*495.4554*) carries clothing for the whole family, their famous rum, nautical items, and island books.

Sea Urchin (*495.4850*) stocks lots and lots of shoes, sandals, bathing suits, beachwear, sundresses, T-shirts, and books. There are two other branches of this terrific store in Road Town.

Xpectations (*495.3446*) is a real one-of-a-kind find. Look for natural herbal soaps, incense, candles, baskets, and exquisite dolls created by the artist/owner and fashioned entirely out of banana leaves

Zenida (*495.4867*) features exotic items from all over the world—colorful fabrics, bedspreads, sarongs, wood carvings, unusual jewelry, carry-alls, and much more.

81

GREAT SHOPPING ELSEWHERE

Aragorn's Studio (*495.1849*), facing Trellis Bay just past the airport, has an elegant display of Caribbean arts and crafts, including island music, unusual pieces of jewelry, artist-designed T-shirts, books, and clothing for women. Dramatic custom-made copper sculptures can be ordered. If you are on island for a while, check out the schedule for pottery, wood carving, basketry, and painting lessons.

Bamboushay (*494.0393*), at Nanny Cay (halfway between Road Town and West End), is where beautiful local pottery is created. Look for stunning bowls, vases, plates, and platters plus paintings by local artists. Anything you buy can be shipped home.

Fluke's Gallery (*495.2043*), facing Trellis Bay just past the airport, is the place to purchase these delightful and well-known island prints.

Long Bay Beach Resort (*495.4252*) has a charming two-story boutique that carries Caribbean art, a wide selection of resortwear and accessories, current books, and handsome T-shirts.

Olivia's Store (*495.9649*), on Cane Garden Bay next to Myett's, is a boutique with many highly original, one-of-a-kind items plus pretty boxes, island artwork, books, T-shirts, sarongs, cover-ups, plus film and suntan lotion.

Skyworld Boutique (*494.3567*), next to Skyworld restaurant (*see page 85*), is tiny but has a bit of everything, from beautiful, locally-made Bamboushay pottery to local artwork to Sunny Caribbee spices.

WHERE TO GO FOR A
GREAT HAIR CUT OR COLOR

The Almond Tree Salon & Day Spa

Make an appointment at the beautifully decorated **Almond Tree Salon & Day Spa**. Year after year owner Janelle Pascoe has been named the best hair stylist and hair colorist in both the USVI and BVI. Come here for a really outstanding haircut—men or women. (*495.4208; closed Sun.; 10 minutes from Road Town and from West End; enter Nanny Cay and follow signs to hotel, drive past hotel, turn right.*)

TORTOLA'S GREAT RESTAURANTS AND BARS

One of the extraordinary things about dining in the islands is that most of the time you are outside. Many restaurants simply don't have walls. A canopy or roof protects you from the occasional cloudburst. In addition, many dining areas overlook the water. It is possible to get anything from a hamburger to an elegant, four course meal in this kind of exotic setting. Restaurants below are organized geographically (See map page 88) and are open daily unless stated otherwise.

IN AND NEAR ROAD TOWN

Brandywine Bay Restaurant (*495.2301*), an easy 10 minute cab ride from Road Town, is set on a hilltop overlooking the water and is the BVI's finest restaurant. Dine by candlelight inside or outside on one of several romantic terraces. Italian owner/chef Davide Pugliese flies in ingredients from all over the world, buys the best local fish, and makes his own mozzarella. Australian owner Cele manages the restaurant and gracefully presents the nightly version of the ever-changing menu, which offers a number of appetizers, entrees, and dessert choices. This is the place to come if you like fresh mussels, beef carpaccio, Peking roast duck with raspberry sauce, grilled filet mignon with porcini mushroom sauce, stuffed veal chops, grilled sushi grade tuna, lemon tarts, and chocolate walnut torte served in an elegant, sophisticated setting. The wine list has excellent Italian and Australian selections. *Casual elegant (long pants, collared shirt for men). Closed early-Aug. to late-Oct. and Sun. D $$$*

C&F (*494.4941*) at Purcell Estate just outside Road Town is run by Clarence, a well-known local chef and his wife, Florence, and it's packed nightly. People come for generous platters of fresh local swordfish and lobster, tasty barbecue ribs, fried plantains, conch fritters, and curry. This is a well-lighted, ultra-casual sort of place, full of diners obviously enjoying their meals. *D $$-$$$*

Capriccio di Mare (*494.5369*), on Waterfront Drive, is an authentic outdoor Italian cafe and the cuisine here is superb. In the morning sip espresso and munch on Italian pastries. Come back around noon and choose from a huge selection of salads, crostinis, focaccia, pastas, and pizzas. Try the Insalata Mista, spaghetti arrabbiati, or spaghetti puttanesca, or penne caprese. Return in the evening for a pizze margherita! The house specialty is a delicious Mango Bellini, a variation of the Bellini cocktail served at Harry's Bar in Venice and there are some good Italian red and white wines. Owners are Davide and Cele Pugliese of Brandywine Bay fame. *Open 8 am-9 pm. Closed Sun. BLD $$*

Captain's Table (*494.3885*), in Road Town on Wickham's Cay I, offers fine dining in a casual setting either inside or outside at the double row of tables along their veranda overlooking the harbor. The tablecloths are red and white checked and the lighting is dim at this popular spot. The French chef has created an outstanding menu of French and Continental selections. In addition to the printed menu there is a blackboard with a huge number of tempting lunch specials and a second blackboard with an equally large number of appealing dinner specials. Choices run the gamut from homemade soups, all kinds of fresh salads, and a multitude of sandwiches and light meals at lunch to vegetarian dishes, veal and chicken creations, grilled steaks, pasta dishes, and much more in the evening—all prepared creatively with fresh ingredients. You can also choose your own fresh live lobster right out of their lobster pool. (Just watch out you don't fall in—the pool is right in the floor in the middle of the dining room.) *L Mon.-Fri., D $$$*

Le Cabanon (*494.8660*), on Waterfront Drive, showcases authentic French fare in a delightful open-air setting. Good lunch choices include the quiche Lorraine with salad and fries, the ham and cheese omelette, the goat cheese salad, the croque monsieur, or the chorizo and brie sandwich. Come back for great dinner selections, which include a grilled filet, duck prepared various ways, and fresh fish. You can't go wrong at this very popular French bistro. *Closed Sun. L(Mon.-Fri.)D $$*

Lime 'n' Mango (*494.2501*), at Treasure Isle Hotel, has a superb view of Road Harbour through the treetops and is a peaceful retreat, especially for breakfast or lunch. Try the lobster salad, club sandwich, or a BLT. *BLD $$*

The Pub (*494.2608*), right across from Fort Burt, has a pleasant veranda overlooking Road Harbour and the views are great day and night. Come to this popular, casual place for barbecued ribs and chicken, sauteed or curried conch, fish and chips, Caesar salad, and burgers and stop by in the morning for great pancakes. *Opens at 5 pm Sun. BLD $$*

Pusser's Pub (*494.3897*) is almost always hopping. Come here for Pusser's famous painkillers plus fish & chips, deli sandwiches, burgers and pizzas. The young crowd heads here every Thursday for "nickel beer night." *LD $-$$*

Roti Palace (*494.4196*), on Main Street in Road Town (above Samarkand), serves up some of the best rotis on the island. (Properly made rotis are curries wrapped in a delicious light and delicate flat bread.) Dine inside or on the cool and breezy hillside veranda and choose from lobster, whelk, conch, beef, or chicken (you'll probably want the boneless). *LD $-$$*

Skyworld (*494.3567*), about 10 minutes straight up from Road Town on Ridge Road, is an elegant spot to dine. Windows in the all-white hexagonal dining room show off stunning views and the cuisine is excellent. Start with warm goat cheese over baby greens or local conch fritters. Move on to chargrilled mahi mahi with pineapple and tequila jus or roast pork tenderloin with Pernod honey-ginger jus or grouper with a guavaberry and tomato cream sauce or macadamia nut-crusted chicken breast. If you care about the view, get here before dark. The lunch menu is much simpler, with pumpkin soup, hamburgers, and sandwiches and salads the fare. *LD $$-$$$*

Spaghetti Junction (*494.4880*), out past the Mill Mall complex, has long been one of Tortola's most popular spots. The second floor dining room is dimly lit and open to the breezes and the most romantic tables look out across Road Harbour. Although this is a casual restaurant, the service, atmosphere, and cuisine are all outstanding, thanks to owners John Schultheiss and April Ridi. Try the delicious bruschetta or tasty mozzarella sticks first. Excellent dinner choices include the shrimp and dill-roasted tomatoes over linguini, spaghetti and meatballs, cioppino (fish stew) over fettuccine, jambalaya pasta, and beef filet with a marsala wine sauce. Save room for the chocolate mousse and some energy for late night partying that goes on at the Bat Cave next door. *Closed Sept. and closed Sun. D $$.*

Virgin Queen (*494.2310*), near the round-a-bout, is where locals and the yachting crowd gather for stouts, ales, and lagers as well as bangers and mash, shepherd's pie, fish and chips, local dishes like salt fish, mutton stew, and peas and rice and their famous Queen's Pizza. *LD $-$$*

WEST END

The "Fish Fry" is on Zion Hill Road on the northwest end of Tortola. This is outdoors and doesn't have a sign, but every Friday and Saturday evening locals stoke up the fires by the side of the road and cook excellent local fish here. It's a minute or so walk from Sebastian's and Little Apple Bay on Tortola's North Shore. *D $*

The Garden (*495.4252*), at Long Bay Beach Resort, offers an elegant setting. Tables are on several levels, all lit by candles and open to the breezes. The menu changes nightly but might include a choice of roasted red pepper soup, salad, or sauteed sea scallops first, then a choice of filet with a port wine sauce, roasted cornish game hen with ratatouille, grilled swordfish, and a vegetarian special. Desserts are a delight, especially the chocolate mousse. You might want to arrive early to enjoy a beverage on the adjoining, very pleasant garden terrace. *Casual elegant. Closed Sun. (also Tues., Fri. off-season) and Sept. D $$$*

85

Jolly Roger (*495.4559*), at West End past the ferry dock, has a delightful open-air terrace and delicious food. Come for a breakfast of French toast, pancakes, or eggs your way. For lunch, the conch fritters, vegetable rotis, and pizzas are excellent choices. At dinner, dine on grilled swordfish or Caribbean jerk prime rib. Weekend nights there's a barbecue. *Closed mid-Aug.-Sept. BLD $-$$*

Mrs. Scatliffe's (*495.4556*) is on Carrot Bay. Known as the queen of local cooking, she serves family style meals in her home every evening. Menus change nightly, but might include curried goat, pot roast pork, chicken and coconut, and conch fritters. *Reservations are necessary by 5:30 pm. D $$*

Nathan's Place (*no phone*), at the west end of Long Bay beach (the last building on the right, before the road turns left), is owned and run by Chef Myra. The surroundings may be very simple and the menu small, but the fare is a treat and includes such local specialties as pumpkin soup and coconut bread, plus burgers and lobster. Don't leave without trying a soursop or mango daiquiri. *Closed Sun. and Sept. LD $-$$*

Pices (*495.3154*), on Frenchman's Cay, has an outdoor terrace and a charming indoor dining room, with pink walls hung with local art. Have a lunch of conch fritters, burgers, Caesar salad, or honey-stung chicken. At dinner, try the curried shrimp, jerk chicken breast, or fresh catch. Breakfast is great, too, from the omelette to eggs Benedict to French toast. *BLD $-$$*

Pusser's Landing (*495.4554*), on Frenchman's Cay, is a popular lunch stop for burgers and pizzas and, of course, Pusser's famous painkillers. *LD $-$$*

Sebastian's On the Beach (*495.4212*), on Apple Bay's north shore, is a great place for breakfast (fresh fruit, eggs, pancakes) or lunch (burgers, sandwiches, conch fritters, chicken or vegetarian rotis, and salads). The terrace overhangs the beach with superb views of pelicans diving for fish. Dinner (grilled lobster, local fish, steaks) is casual but romantic. *Call ahead for lobster. BLD $-$$*

Sugar Mill (*495.4355*), in Apple Bay, is a romantic spot. The setting is lovely, in a restored 360-year-old sugar mill with beautiful stonework walls and tables lit by candles. The menu changes nightly, with a choice of several appetizers, salads, entrees, and desserts. Black bean and roasted pumpkin soup, Hoisin duck in a scallion pancake, and chipotle chicken sausage are typical appetizers, and for the main course, grilled local fish with mango salsa, filet mignon with sun-dried tomato Bernaise sauce, mustard-crusted rack of lamb, and a vegetarian dish such as pumpkin and black bean lasagna. Come early for a drink in the lovely outdoor gazebo. *Smart casual (dress shorts okay for men). Closed Aug.-Sept. D $$-$$$*

CANE GARDEN BAY

Myett's Garden and Grill (*495.9649*), on the beach at Cane Garden Bay, is a casual, barefoot sort of place. Burgers, salads, and excellent vegetarian rotis are good lunch choices. Dinner features ribs, chicken, and lobster. *LD $-$$*

Big Banana Club Paradise (*495.4606*), on the beach at Cane Garden Bay, serves sandwiches, pizza, ice cream, and great island drinks. *LD $-$$*

Quito's Gazebo (*495.4837*), at the east end of Cane Garden Bay, is owned by recording star Quito Rhymer and is a good place to come for burgers and rotis at lunch and ribs, conch, and fresh local fish West Indian style for dinner. Tuesday and Thursday evenings, Quito performs solo and Friday and Saturday nights he entertains with his band. *LD $-$$*

EAST END AND TRELLIS BAY

De Loose Mongoose (*495.2303*), on the beach at Trellis Bay, is ultra-casual and great for tasty pumpkin soup, burgers, rotis, sandwiches, and frozen island drinks, all served at blue picnic tables inside and out. *Closed Mon. BLD $-$$*

Eclipse (*495.1646*), at Penn's Landing, in an elegant setting over the water, features an eclectic menu: spring rolls, quesadillas, chicken skewers jerk Jamaican or Thai-seared, lobster ravioli, polenta with shitake mushrooms and sun-dried tomatoes, or sesame tuna carpaccio. Many items are also available in small portions, so you can "graze" through dinner, ordering one at a time (some smalls are on the large size, so let the knowledgeable waitstaff be your guide). Flight afficianodoes will enjoy watching the little planes in final approach. *Closed Mon.; Sun. open for brunch only. D, Sun. Brunch $$-$$$*

Fat Hog Bob's (*495.1010*) is in Maya Cove. Beer banners hang from the ceiling at this appealing and spacious bar and restaurant, with handsome wood walls, a terrace overlooking the water, and the wine list on the table lampshades. Come here when you need an "Outback" fix: bloomin' onions and piles of french fries plus giant burgers, steaks, ribs, and local fish. *LD $$-$$$*

Tamarind Club (*495.2477*) sits high above Josiah's Bay and is very popular and worth a visit despite its somewhat remote location. Tables are spread about on a large open-air terrace and the evening's ample number of selections are inscribed on a blackboard brought to your seat. Starters might include a pumpkin bacon soup, Chef Mo's crab cakes, and a sesame ginger calamari and seaweed salad. The main courses could be filet mignon with a goat cheese and red wine sauce, rack of lamb with basil almond pesto crust, and seared sesame-crusted tuna with wasabi aioli. *BLD, Sun. Brunch $$-$$$*

BEYOND TORTOLA'S EAST END

Pusser's Marina Cay (*494.2174*) has free ferry service (*schedules page 140*) from their dock on Beef Island to their restaurant on Marina Cay. The dinner menu features barbecue ribs, grilled steak, lobster, and fresh fish served in their al fresco beachside restaurant. *LD $$*

The Last Resort (*495.2520*) is actually on a tiny little islet just off Beef Island. Not only is there an eclectic menu of tapas, local seafood, and roast beef, there's also Tony Snell's popular, after-dinner show. *D $$*

to Pusser's Marina Cay
& The Last Resort

TORTOLA'S
RESTAURANTS

De Loose Mongoose

BEEF I.

Eclipse
Fat Hog Bob's

Tamarind Club

Brandywine Bay

Skyworld

ROAD TOWN

Quito's Gazebo
Big Banana
Myett's

Mrs. Scatliffe's
Sugar Mill
"Fish Fry"
Sebastian's
The Garden
Nathan's Place

Pices

Jolly Roger

Pusser's Landing

Restaurants in Roadtown
C&F
Capriccio di Mare
Captain's Table
Le Cabanon
Lime 'n' Mango
The Pub
Pusser's Pub
Roti Palace
Spaghetti Junction
Virgin Queen

⇐ N

SOME TIPS ON BVI RESTAURANTS

❏Don't be alarmed if there aren't many other patrons in a restaurant. In the U.S. this generally means that you are in a bad place, but in the islands it is perfectly normal. In the islands there are just far fewer people around.

❏Contrary to popular thought, vegetables and fruits are not plentiful on these islands. (The rains are too uneven and the land too rocky.) Virtually all produce is shipped from the southern Caribbean, Puerto Rico, or from the States. If there is very little lettuce in your salad, it is probably because the restaurant is desperately waiting for a fresh shipment to come in.

❏Fresh milk is shipped from St. Thomas and Puerto Rico and quickly turns in the Caribbean heat. Although you will see fresh milk in the supermarkets, virtually everyone relies on "Long Life" milk which comes in non-refrigerated cartons and is usually from England.

❏Many visitors from the U.S. get frustrated by the peaceful pace of restaurant service, forgetting, of course, that the reason they came to the BVI in the first place was to slow down and relax. Enjoy the scenery and the pace. If you have to catch a plane or a boat, let someone know and they'll happily serve you more quickly.

❏Water is scarce on these islands. Islanders can last a week with the water people from the U.S. can waste in a day. Drinking water is rarely served unless requested.

❏Many restaurants serve American-style food, but it won't necessarily be exactly what you are expecting. Cooking styles are different here and supplies are limited.

GREAT NIGHTLIFE ON TORTOLA

On Friday and Saturday nights and Sunday afternoons many Tortola bars and restaurants feature live entertainment. However, you can usually find live music any night of the week, especially on season. BVI musicians often play at a different hotel or bar each night, so if you find a group you particularly like, find out where they will be playing next.

Many musicians travel back and forth between the islands but no one beats guitarist Ruben Chinnery, who often entertains on several islands in the course of a single afternoon and evening.

One of the great things about all of this music is that generally you are listening to it outside, under the blanket of Caribbean stars! Remember, bands do move around, so it's best to call the establishment to see which band will be there or to check the Limin' Times, *which comes out weekly, for up-to-the-minute schedules of who is playing where.*

Love Songs

For romantic sounds, be sure to find wonderful Ruben Chinnery, who hails from Jost Van Dyke and who plays the guitar and sings ballads and love songs. Or check out Quito, who plays love songs at his own restaurant in Cane Garden Bay, Quito's Gazebo.

Steel Bands

Do catch a steel band at least once—the music is quite beautiful and it's hard to believe these smooth mellow sounds are made by striking oil drums. This form of music originated in Trinidad but is now found all over the Caribbean. Great BVI steel bands include Pan-Vibes and the Shooting Stars and Clem's.

Fungi Bands

Fungi bands are a type of scratch band that combines flutes with washboards, bottles, gourds, and other household items. It's hard not to get caught up in the fun and rhythm of a fungi band! See if you can find the fungi bands Spark Plugs or Romeo and the Injectors.

Reggae

O-2B and Third Dimension play a kind of modernized Reggae plus contempory top-40s and rock and roll—all great for shaking-it-up or dancing cheek-to-cheek.

TORTOLA NIGHTLIFE

Bat Cave (*next to Spaghetti Junction in Road Town, 494.4880*). The bar and three decks are jam-packed nightly at Tortola's hottest night spot. There's usually live entertainment Wednesdays and weekends.

Bomba's Shack (*Apple Bay, North Shore, 495.4148*). Local bands play here Wednesday evenings and Sunday afternoons and at his famous all-night Full Moon and Blue Moon Parties.

Fat Hog Bob's (*Maya Cove, 495.1010*) features bands Friday nights.

Jolly Roger. (*West End, 495.4559*). Come for live bands and a barbecue every Friday and Saturday (and sometimes Thursday).

Long Bay Beach Resort (*Long Bay, North Shore, 495.4252*). The Tuesday night barbecue features the steel band Pan-Vibes and the Third Dimension plays at the Friday barbecue.

Myett's (*Cane Garden Bay, 495.9649*). Friday, Saturday, Sunday, and Monday nights local bands keep this popular spot hopping.

The Pub (*Road Town, 494.2608*). Ruben Chinnery entertains here Friday evenings.

Quito's Gazebo (*Cane Garden Bay, North Shore, 495.4837*). Recording star Quito Rhymer plays guitar and sings his love songs and ballads every night but Monday and Wednesday. There are also local bands here on weekends.

Sebastian's (*Apple Bay, North Shore, 495.4212*). Frequently a local band plays here on weekends. Often, Saturday night it's the steel band Pan-Vibes, and Sunday it's the fungi band The Spark Plugs.

BOMBA'S SHACK

Most everybody has heard of Bomba by now. His Full Moon Parties are famous throughout the Caribbean. Drive by the place during the day and you might mistake it for a junk pile, but Wednesdays, Sundays, and full moon nights the place, and the beach and fields around it, are packed. You can stop here any day any time after 10 am and try Bomba's specialty, a blend of passionfruit, guava, banana, papaya, pineapple, and orange juices mixed with Bomba's homemade rum—a secret recipe handed down by his family.

WONDERFUL SIGHTS AT NIGHT

Shooting stars. Just stare at the night sky for a few minutes and you're bound to catch a shooting star. Some shooting stars streak high across the sky but others are so big and fall so close they'll take your breath away.

Satellites. Stare up at the sky and watch for a satellite. This can take some patience, but eventually you will see one making its way across the nighttime canopy. It will look like an airplane way up high, but without the telltale red and green blinking lights.

Southern Cross. Many think this is visible only from the southern hemisphere but in June and July, especially if you are on a hilltop in the BVI looking south, you can catch this legendary constellation just above the horizon. There's no mistaking this one when you see it.

Glitter in the water. Catch the sparkling phosphorescence. Streak a stick through the water at the edge of a dark dock, or watch your paddle stir up glitter on a nighttime kayak ride, or watch water gently lapping against the shore, especially on a moonless night when there is less competing light.

Underwater Sights. Go on a night dive or a night snorkel. It's completely different than a daytime underwater adventure and truly unbelievable to see how many "electric" creatures dance around in the nighttime ocean.

DON'T MISS . . .

❑Dinner at Brandywine Bay Restaurant

❑Stopping by Bamboushay to see the beautiful pottery that is handcrafted on site

❑A visit to at least one Pusser's store

❑Joining in the after-dinner fun and festivities at the popular Bat Cave

❑At least one snorkel, anywhere

❑Browsing through one (or all) of the Sea Urchin shops for great swimwear, casual clothing, sandals, and souvenirs

❑The view from Skyworld

❑A cappuccino or a Mango Bellini or a bowl of penne with spicy tomato sauce at Capriccio di Mare in Road Town

❑Taking at least one nautical adventure, from renting a dinghy to going on a day sail

❑Breakfast at Sebastian's, watching the pelicans dive-bomb for their morning repast

❑Dinner at elegant Sugar Mill or Long Bay's Garden Restaurant

TORTOLA'S GREAT LODGING CHOICES

Bear in mind that BVI resorts are in scale with the islands and quite small compared to those in the U.S. A full-service resort in the U.S. might have 1,000 rooms and, in fact, there are less than 1,000 hotel rooms in all of the British Virgin Islands. Also, in the BVI, as on most islands, many "expected" services such as room service or dry cleaning usually aren't available (there is only one dry cleaner in the BVI). The trade-off for this lack of "services" is an extraordinary peace and quiet, an incredibly relaxed pace, and truly empty beaches.

Rates are per night for two people without meals on season, and do not include service charge (usually 10%) and 7% government tax. Prices ranges reflect different levels of accommodations. Off-season rates are in parentheses.

West End Lodging
FORT RECOVERY ESTATE

Pamelah Jacobson makes this cozy spot what it is—a great place to chill out, cool down, and simply recover from the stresses of stateside life.

Right on a smallish beach five minutes from West End by car is this very casual mini-resort that looks out toward Frenchman's Cay and St. John in the USVI. You drive through a gate and slip into a private and relaxing world full of brilliant tropical flowers. There is one beachfront three-bedroom villa, a two-bedroom villa, a one-bedroom poolside villa, and two floors of comfortable one-and two-bedroom apartments facing the water. These are staggered so that balconies are fairly private. Interiors are bright and designed to be easy to live in, with small but full kitchens, air-conditioned bedrooms, separate living areas, and TVs. Penthouse apartments are on the second floor and have beamed cathedral ceilings and an airy feel. VCRs and videos are available for rent. Rates include a continental breakfast with delicious homemade breads. Although there is no restaurant, dinner can be served to you in your living room or on your terrace, course by course. The beach is smallish but very calm and good for swimming and snorkeling and there is a dock and an appealing swimming pool. Water sports, yoga, and massage therapy are available on-site and boat trips can be arranged.

17 units. Rates for one-bedroom units (with continental breakfast): $230-$265 ($145-$170). Reservations Manager: Pamelah Jills Jacobson. Reservations: 800.367.8455. Tel: 284.495.4354. Fax: 284.495.4036. P.O. Box 239. Web: www.fortrecovery.com

LONG BAY BEACH RESORT & VILLAS

A spectacular mile-long beach, two pools, tennis courts, two appealing restaurants, a full-service spa, and great accommodations make this 52-acre resort (which is the closest to a full-service resort on Tortola) a place you may never want to leave, but it's also a great location if you want to explore—it's easy to go to Smuggler's Cove or West End or even to hop over to Jost Van Dyke.

Tucked behind the sea grape trees along the beach are cozy rooms on stilts and also spacious deluxe units with large balconies and walk-in showers. Sea grapes are between these deluxe units and the beach and the second-floor units have better views. Scattered up the hillside are studios with jacuzzis, poolside studios (top floor units have cathedral ceilings and feel more spacious), and one-, two-, and three-bedroom villas with full kitchens. The hillside is steep and views from most of the poolside and hillside units are stunning (and the walk back and forth from the beach or dinner is superb exercise). Units have air-conditioned bedrooms, phones, coffee makers, refrigerators, and TVs. The Garden Restaurant (*see page 85*) is an excellent choice for dinner, the casual Beach Restaurant is open for all meals, and there's a poolside snack bar. There are two pools (one with a swim-up bar), an informal 9-hole pitch & putt course, three tennis courts, a neat boutique, a full-service spa (for massages, mud wraps, and more), and a commissary.

115 units. Rates: $275-$545 ($155-$225), villas more. General Manager: Bernd Gable. Reservations: 800.729.9599. Tel: 284.495.4252. Fax 284.495.4677. P.O.Box 433. Web: www.longbay.com.

SEBASTIAN'S SEASIDE VILLAS

Look out at great views of azure water and Caribbean islands and pelicans diving for dinner from these upscale and comfortable efficiencies built right above the water's edge and near an excellent casual restaurant.

These nine efficiencies are in a two-story building that overlooks the water just past the edge of narrow Apple Bay beach. All units are nicely decorated with dark wood furniture, pale yellow walls, and framed prints and have contemporary marble bathrooms and a cozy kitchenette with toaster, microwave, sink, and little fridge. Sliding glass doors stretch the length of the room, showcase stunning views, and open onto a private narrow balcony. The second story rooms have cathedral ceilings and feel especially spacious. All units have ceiling fans, air-conditioning, and cable TV.

Sebastian's restaurant (*see page 86*) is a delightful stop for breakfast, lunch, and dinner and there is also a bar and live entertainment some nights. A little commissary next to reception carries the basics. Sebastian's also has 12 small beachfront rooms that are very basically furnished but can be a good value. Call for rates. By the way, Sebastian's is a short walk from Bomba's Shack, and you should stay here during a full moon only if you want to be part of Bomba's Full Moon Party.

9 units. Rates: $300 ($200-$275), two-bedroom suite $550 ($350-$500). General Manager: Uschi Mikoleiczik. Tel: 284.495.4212. Fax: 284.4954466. P.O. Box 441. Web: www.sebastiansvillas.com

THE SUGAR MILL

Stay here when you want a simple yet sophisticated hideaway with a little patch of beach and an excellent restaurant. You can spend your days reading and resting or use it as a cozy base from which to explore.

Comfortable rooms, cooled by ceiling fans and air-conditioning, spill down the hillside at this intimate north shore spot not far from West End. Each has a little kitchen with a fridge and microwave and private balconies look out to the ocean through the trees. There are also two spacious two-bedroom Plantation House Suites (the upstairs one has a cathedral ceiling) and a two-bedroom villa with a full kitchen. Suites and the villa have TV and VCRs. A 360-year-old sugar mill with handsome stone walls provides the appealing setting for reception, casual breakfasts, a little bar, and fine dining in the well-known Sugar Mill, open for dinner only and one of the best restaurants on the island (*see page 86*). Islands, a little beach grill, serves burgers, salads, and West Indian dishes for lunch and, Tuesday through Saturday on season, also offers West-Indian inspired selections for dinner. The petite beach across the street is calm and good for swimming and snorkeling (there's a reef right at the end). Because it's tiny it's private, as non-guests rarely stop here. You can also take a dip in the circular pool.

Closed Aug., Sept. 24 units, including 2 villas. Rates: rooms $215-310 ($180-$225), suites $635 ($490), villa $620 ($475). General Manager: Patrick Conway. Reservations: 800.462.8834. Tel: 284.495-4355. Fax: 284.495.4696. P.O. Box 425. Web: www.sugarmillhotel.com

Cane Garden Bay Lodging
THE OLE WORKS INN

The location on Cane Garden Bay is the draw here.

Rooms are modest but Tortola's most famous beach is across the street and can be your playground day and night. The main building is a 300-year-old restored sugar factory. Some units look out to the beach and others into the hills. There is also a simple honeymoon tower and a small swimming pool.

18 units. Rates: $95-$130 ($60-$85). Owner: Quito Rhymer. Tel: 284.495.4837. Fax 284.495.9618. P.O. Box 560. Web: www.bviguide.com/ole.html

Brewer's Bay Lodging
ICIS VILLAS

Located in a beautiful green valley a short walk from Brewer's Bay, this remote and comfortable hideaway with its own restaurant is a good choice for couples or families or anyone seeking isolation and a great beach.

Brewer's Bay is one of the more difficult places to get to on Tortola (lots of steep hills and unmarked roads) and it is a surprise to find this delightful oasis tucked in the greenery a short walk from the western edge of Brewer's Bay beach. The grounds are stunning, with lush tropical foliage, 60-year-old mahogany trees, and 100-year-old mango trees. The restaurant, small commissary, and reception are built around the remains of the first Baptist church to be built in the BVI and the ancient stone walls are remarkable. Units are in a two-story motel-like structure but inside you will find comfortable one-, two-, and three-bedroom suites. All have air-conditioned bedrooms, separate living/dining areas with full kitchens, cable TV, and a terrace or balcony. There are also two efficiencies, each with a fully-equipped kitchen. Spend the day relaxing by the waterfall and lovely landscaped pool or take the three-minute walk to the beach. The hotel restaurant does not serve lunch but there's a restaurant at the beach that does. *15 units. Rates: $145-$185 ($125-$155), two-bedroom deluxe $290 ($230). General Manager: Allison Roddy. Tel: 284.494.6769. Fax: 284.494.6980. P.O. Box 383. Web: www.icisvillas.com*

East End Lodging
LAMBERT BEACH RESORT

The beach is long and beautiful at this quiet and peaceful resort nestled between the water and the hills on Tortola's north shore.

Although close to East End and the airport, this resort is over some hills and on its own half mile of beach and is fairly remote (which makes stargazing from the beach here outstanding because it's so dark at night). The grounds are lush and rooms and suites are in one-story white stucco buildings with barrel tile roofs scattered along the waterfront rim of the property. Beach Front Rooms are closest to the water, Ocean View Rooms face the water but are set back, and Garden View Rooms look out to tropical foliage. All units are decorated in print fabrics, have large showers, sliding glass doors that open out to a patio, and air-conditioning. Suites have a separate living room. There's an open-air restaurant, a tennis court, a clubhouse with satellite TV, and an enormous swimming pool, by far the BVI's largest (which non-guests can use for a fee). *38 units. Rates: $160-$250 ($100-170), suites more. General Manager: Yonaho Leslie. Tel: 284.495.2877. Fax 284.495.2876. P.O. Box 534. Web: www.lambertbeachresort.com*

TAMARIND CLUB HOTEL

Nestled in the hills above remote Josiah's Bay beach is this somewhat rustic retreat with a popular bar and excellent restaurant.

This compact little hideaway is built into the hills high above Josiah's Bay. The pool is sort of the geographical center, with rooms at either end, and the bar and open-air library/common room right alongside the pool. (Swim under the bridge to the swim-up side of the bar). Some units are in a two-story white building with arches framing the verandas and others are in a one-story building on the other side of the pool. The nine units are of various sizes, rustically built, and very simply decorated but each has a little fridge and all are air-conditioned. The isolated beach is close to a mile downhill but it is pretty easy to catch a ride back up if you don't have a car. The popular restaurant (*see page 87*) turns out excellent cuisine.

9 rooms. Rates (including continental breakfast): $100-$150 ($80-$110). General Manager: Dawn Rosenberg. Tel: 284.495-2477. Fax 284.495.2795. P.O. Box 509. Web: www.tamarindclub.com

Road Town Lodging
TREASURE ISLE HOTEL

When you want to stay in Road Town, this hillside hotel with a pretty pool and bar and restaurant with a view is a good choice.

Most rooms are in a two-story building and those on the second floor have cathedral ceilings and feel more spacious. Other units are scattered up the hill. All are simply decorated, air-conditioned, and comfortable but not luxurious. Bathrooms are basic. There's a free-form pool (windows at the hotel entrance look right into the depths of the pool), an al fresco restaurant that feels as if it is up in the trees, and a pleasant large open-air lounge and bar that looks out to the harbour and the Moorings marina. When you stay here, you can sit by the pool or walk across to the Moorings bar and restaurant and marina or walk five minutes to town and its various restaurants and bars.

40 rooms. Rates: $167-$253 ($104-$137). General Manager: Al Henley. Tel: 284.494.2501. Fax 284.494.2507. P.O. Box 509. Web: www.treasure islehotel.net

"I never met a place like this in my life."

—Author Hugh Benjamin,
upon his arrival to the BVI

TORTOLA LODGING

BEEF I.

Lambert Beach Resort

Tamarind Club Hotel

Treasure Isle Hotel

ROAD TOWN AND HARBOUR

Icis Villas

TORTOLA

Ole Works Inn

The Sugar Mill

Fort Recovery Estates

Sebastian's
Seaside Villas

Long Bay
Beach
Resort

⇐ N

MORE THINGS PEOPLE USUALLY WISH THEY HAD KNOWN SOONER

❑September is exceptionally slow and some resorts and restaurants close up. Some stay closed through mid-October. Tortola is the least shut-down island (only a handful of restaurants and resorts actually close) but Virgin Gorda is exceptionally quiet during this time and almost nothing is open on Jost Van Dyke. The advantage of traveling this time of year is that you have the beaches and roads to yourself.

❑When you fly from Puerto Rico to the BVI you are almost always over islands and you really get to see how close everything is. If you are flying on American Eagle, generally the best views are out of the right side of the plane (and the left side going home). You'll get a sense of how these politically separated islands are actually one long string of hills poking out of the sea.

❑You'll see goats, cows, roosters, horses, and an occasional pig on roads and also in town. Contrary to popular opinion, roosters not only crow at dawn but whenever they bloody well feel like it, which is pretty much 24/7 and why some people prefer air-conditioning despite the beautiful breezes.

❑Jost Van Dyke is more crowded on weekends because day-trippers come from St. Thomas.

❑To the delight of taxi drivers and the dismay of almost everyone else, from November to April cruise ships disgorge passengers onto Tortola several days a week and they spill into Road Town, Sage Mountain, Skyworld, and Cane Garden Bay. (Check the paper for cruise ship schedules if you want to avoid these crowds).

CYBER CAFES, THE INTERNET, AND E-MAIL

Even though phone service (expecially long distance) can be difficult in the BVI, you can get online at most hotels, either in your room or in the lobby, if you have a laptop. Some hotels also have a guest computer in the lobby. In addition, there are a number of Cyber Cafes and many bars and restaurants have a computer you can log onto. Some of the places you can get connected are listed below.

JOST VAN DYKE
Christine's Bakery, just past the Customs Office, has connections.

TORTOLA
Click Online Cyber Cafe.
Located on the marina side of the Mill Mall Complex in downtown Road Town, this is the place to come for coffee and juice and to settle down at the computer.

Trellis Bay Cyber Cafe.
Stop here to catch up on e-mail or browse the internet. Computer terminals are inside, along with comfortable couches and magazines. Stay for a delicious sandwich on the breezy deck or relax in the hammock. It's on Beef Island at Trellis Bay, a short walk from the airport.

The Pub (across the street from Fort Burt just east of Road Town) and **Fat Hog Bob's** (in East End at Maya Cove) both have computer terminals you can use.

VIRGIN GORDA
Stop by the **Leverick Bay Resort** or the **Bitter End Yacht Club** in North Sound.

MUSEUMS AND RUINS

Around the islands you will find a few museums and ruins of forts and a copper mine. Displays are small and informal but often quite interesting.

TORTOLA
Fort Burt.
The Dutch constructed this fort to guard the mouth of Road Town Harbour and the British rebuilt it in the late 1600s. Now the remains form the foundation for a bar with a spacious terrace and a stunning view.

Fort Recovery.
Built by the Dutch in 1660, this turreted gun emplacement has walls that are three feet thick. It's the oldest intact structure in the BVI.

Government House.
A little museum displays various documents including a handwritten account of one person's experiences during the hurricane of 1924 and signatures of Queen Elizabeth II and the Queen Mother in the Visitor's Book. There are cannonballs, glass bottles, murals, and more, plus a small gift shop.

Mount Healthy National Park.
Here you'll find the remains of a stone windmill, part of a sugar plantaion dating from the 18th century.

VIRGIN GORDA
The Coppermine (at Coppermine Point, The Valley).
Come here to see the remains of a chimney, mine shafts, and a boiler house used by Cornish miners searching for copper in the mid-1800s.

11. VIRGIN GORDA

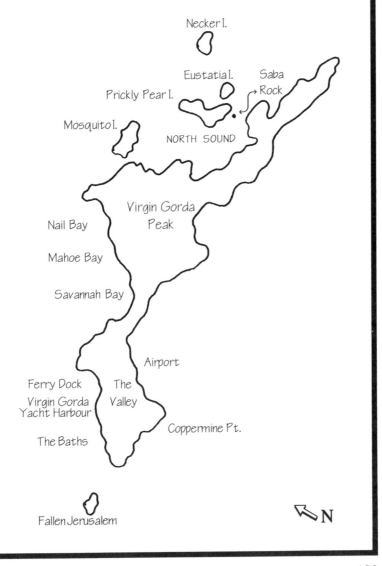

Necker I.

Eustatia I.

Saba Rock

Prickly Pear I.

Mosquito I.

NORTH SOUND

Virgin Gorda Peak

Nail Bay

Mahoe Bay

Savannah Bay

Airport

Ferry Dock

The Valley

Virgin Gorda Yacht Harbour

Coppermine Pt.

The Baths

Fallen Jerusalem

N

VIRGIN GORDA IN A NUTSHELL

Slender Virgin Gorda is 10 miles long and lies seven miles east of Tortola. Only 3,174 people live there, but it's the second most populated British Virgin Island. A big mountain in the middle divides the island into two separate destinations: the Valley and North Sound. These two areas are somewhat isolated from each other and geographically dissimilar and visiting these two places are completely different experiences.

The Valley

The southern end of Virgin Gorda, referred to as the Valley or Spanish Town, is rather flat and strewn with giant boulders. The famous Baths are here, as are several other small and lovely beaches. You'll also find a luxury resort, villa rentals and villa rental complexes, restaurants and bars and, at the Virgin Gorda Yacht Harbour, a small cluster of shops. This part of Virgin Gorda is fairly compact, with places to go and stay within a few easy minutes of each other. Just north of the Valley, along the western shore of the mountain that divides the island, there is an additional hotel and several villa rental complexes connected by a road to the Valley. When you want to go anywhere in this part of Virgin Gorda, you walk or drive or taxi across land, the way you do on most islands.

North Sound

An extremely steep road leads up over the top of Virgin Gorda's mountain and drops precipitously down to North Sound. Here, the long and curvy northern shore of Virgin Gorda, along with the shores of Mosquito and Prickly Pear Islands, almost completely encircles the remarkable North Sound, one of the world's most protected sounds.

Resorts are scattered around the hilly rim of North Sound. With the exception of one hotel and villa complex, these resorts are accessible only by boat. A handful of restaurants and little shops also are scattered along the shores and almost all of these, too, are not reachable by road. To get almost anywhere in North Sound, instead of traveling across land you travel back and forth across water, either via water taxi or your own little boat. It can be delightful to experience life without cars.

PART 1: THE VALLEY

Note: This chapter on Virgin Gorda is divided into two sections: The Valley, which begins here, and North Sound, which begins on page 121.

WHAT YOU CAN DO IN THE VALLEY

You can rent a villa or stay in a luxury resort or a comfortable hotel room. Head to the The Baths and frolic among the boulders and hike or snorkel to several other nearby boulder-filled beaches. Take a picnic to Coppermine Point, a ruin of a copper mine on a windswept rocky point. Hike to the top of Gorda Peak. Visit the delightful nature center. Rent a boat for the day or take a boat trip. Then catch your breath and relax at one of the area's mostly casual but excellent restaurants.

GETTING TO THE VALLEY FROM NEARBY ISLANDS OR NORTH SOUND

You can reach the Valley on Virgin Gorda by public ferry from Road Town on Tortola or Trellis Bay on Beef Island or Charlotte Amalie on St. Thomas (*see Appendix for ferry schedules on page 138*). From Virgin Gorda's North Sound, you can drive or taxi from Leverick Bay or Gun Creek. For information on arriving from the U.S. or U.K. see page 135.

EXPLORING THE VALLEY

The whole southern end of Virgin Gorda is strewn with giant, smooth-sided boulders. On land, they form remarkable natural sculptures. In the water, they create dramatic pools and secret grottoes. The Baths, Virgin Gorda's most famous landmark, is a stunning showcase for these boulder clusters but you will see them at other beaches as well.

The Virgin Gorda Yacht Harbour is the "hub" of the Valley. Beaches are to the south and north, along the western edge of the island. Coppermine Point is on the southeastern tip of Virgin Gorda. The Baths and other beaches south of Yacht Harbour, the snorkeling areas, and Coppermine Point are the all part of the BVI National Parks Trust, a system of protected water and land areas. Please respect signs and don't leave anything behind but your footprints.

Renting a jeep or hiring a taxi

You can rent a car or jeep for $50-$60 a day from **L & S Jeep Rental and Taxi** (*495.5297*), **Mahogany Car Rentals and Taxi** (*495.5469*), or **Speedy's** (*495.5240*). You can get a taxi at the airport, at the ferry dock, or at the Taxi Stand in the parking lot south of the Yacht Harbour from these same three outfits. To be picked up, for either a taxi or a car rental, just call. Taxis vary from brightly-striped, canopied, open "safari buses" to jeep-type vehicles to regular sedans. The fare to anywhere from anywhere in the Valley (Savannah Bay and south) is $2 to $4 per person. Drivers are happy to drop you at the beach and pick you up later. It's $24 for up to four people to Nail Bay or Gun Creek or Leverick Bay. An hour-and-a-half island tour is about $35 for two people.

SHORTCUT FROM THE FERRIES
TO THE YACHT HARBOUR

Public ferries arrive just north of the Virgin Gorda Yacht Harbour. Taxis meet the ferries and friendly drivers will take you anywhere but if you want to see the Yacht Harbour first, you can easily walk. Go past the ferry terminal, turn right into the parking lot, and head toward the large field bordered by a chain-link fence (don't worry, it's public property). You'll see a path that leads from an opening in the fence. Follow it and in a minute or two you'll be right at Yacht Harbour.

VISITING THE BATHS, OTHER BEACHES, AND COPPERMINE POINT

THE BATHS, DEVIL'S BAY, SPRING BAY, THE CRAWL, LITTLE TRUNK BAY, AND BIG TRUNK BAY

Virgin Gorda's southwest shore is laced with one white sandy crescent of beach after another, each separated by clusters of giant rocky boulders. The scenery here is simply stunning: glistening sand, water in a thousand shades of blue, shapely islands in the distance. Narrow and often hilly walking paths connect the beaches but it is also possible to snorkle from beach to beach when the water is calm. These are superb beaches for swimming and snorkeling. The water is usually calm and always extraordinarily clear.

The Baths. This is Virgin Gorda's most celebrated landmark and, along with The Crawl, is one of the best spots to experience swimming in the pools and grottoes created by the boulders. The Baths is extremely popular but still definitely worth a visit. To avoid the crowds come early or late in the day. The path, which takes about 10 minutes to walk, starts at the circle where you park your car. It's clearly etched into the ground and drops gently, curving around giant boulders. At the beach, you'll find the Poor Man's Bar, a good stop for cold drinks, hot dogs, and sandwiches, plus T-shirts and rental snorkel gear. There are lockers for rent, public restrooms, and a tiny gift shop open whimsical hours.

Devil's Bay. It's just south of The Baths and the most appealing and adventurous route starts at The Baths. Head to the south end of the beach and look for the sign and the narrow space at the bottom of two boulders. Stoop down and head through the space. Be prepared to, as the sign says, "crawl, climb ladders, and wade through water" to get to the next beach. This approach to Devil's Bay takes about 20 minutes. You can come back the way you came or take the land path back from Devil's Bay to the parking circle. You can also start with the land path (it's about a-15 minute walk) and make this trip in reverse and on calm days you can also snorkel from one beach to the other.

Spring Bay. Actually two beaches separated by a few rocks, this is the next beach north of The Baths and far less crowded.

The Crawl. Just north of Spring Bay is this remarkable natural pool formed by giant boulders. The water is extra calm and shallow here and this is a great place for novice snorkelers to practice. A sign marks the entrance to the road leading to the parking lot. From there it's a five-minute walk to the beach. Or you can follow the narrow curvy and hilly path from Spring Bay or Little Trunk Bay.

Little Trunk Bay and Big Trunk Bay. These are the next two beaches north of the Crawl and are connected by little paths but not accessible from the road.

SAVANNAH BAY BEACHES AND POND BAY BEACH
When you are in the mood for a fabulous stretch of beach that is also often deserted, head to the Savannah Bay Beaches and Pond Bay Beach, which are an easy 10 minutes north of the Virgin Gorda Yacht Harbour. Savannah Bay Beach is over half a mile long. Pond Bay Beach and Little Savannah Bay Beach are smaller beaches. The sand here is stunningly white, the waters multihued, and the reef makes anchorages difficult so few people approach from the water. To get to **Savannah Bay Beach**, go past the Olde Yard Village and then over a hill and then look for a turn-off on the left just when the road flattens out. There's a sign there but it's facing the other way. Follow the turn-off to the parking area and then follow the short path to the beach. To get to **Little Savannah Bay Beach**, follow the path at the south end of Savannah Bay Beach. There is a path from the road to **Pond Bay Beach** but it is difficult to see. Drive past the Savannah Bay entrance and you should see the path on the left just before you get to the left turn to Nail Bay. Park along the roadside.

COPPERMINE POINT
Coppermine Point is a rocky spit of land facing west and the prevailing winds stir up the surf. Come here for a great view of crashing waves and to walk among the ruins of an old copper mine. To get there, turn right out of the Yacht Harbour parking lot and take the first left after the round-about and drive until this road ends at a "T." Turn right and stay on this road to the end. The road can be very bouncy and you may feel lost, but stick with it for 10 minutes and you'll arrive.

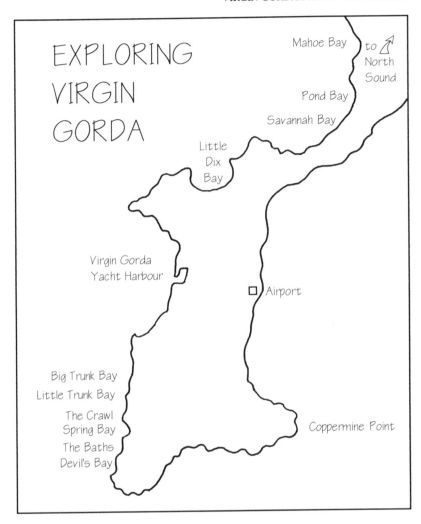

EXPLORING VIRGIN GORDA

Mahoe Bay

to North Sound

Pond Bay

Savannah Bay

Little Dix Bay

Virgin Gorda Yacht Harbour

☐ Airport

Big Trunk Bay
Little Trunk Bay
The Crawl
Spring Bay
The Baths
Devil's Bay

Coppermine Point

SNORKELING AND DIVING FROM THE VALLEY

All beaches in the Valley have good snorkeling. If you need equipment (mask, fins, snorkel), you can sometimes rent it from your hotel or you can rent it at The Baths or you can rent or buy equipment from **DIVE BVI** (*495.5513*) at Virgin Gorda Yacht Harbour. Divers can call Dive BVI for half-day and full-day diving trips, night dives, and resort courses. If you want to go on a boat rip that includes a bit of snorkeling, see page 111.

109

GREAT THINGS TO DO ON VIRGIN GORDA

Treat yourself to the lunch buffet at Little Dix Resort (*495.5555*). Seating is under a stunning arch that frames a gorgeous view. The cuisine is a delight, too. Plates and plates of composed salads plus fruits, cheeses, and desserts and, for an additional charge, burgers, dogs, and various entrees.

Go to the airport. Watch the little planes land on the tiny strip of dirt Virgin Gordans call a runway. Passengers get out of the planes looking startled, especially when they realize they've been part of the show!

Rent a dinghy and explore North Sound. You can spend the day putt-putting about or you can snorkel over the side or you can just drift about and take in the scenery.

Go floating. Get on one of those yellow or blue floats and just lie there. If you are into decadent snorkeling bring your mask, hang your head over the end, and gaze underwater. Otherwise just lie there and float. It's so relaxing.

Head to Biras Creek Resort for a sweeping sunset view over cocktails and an elegant dinner. Call ahead (*494.3555*) and they'll pick you up free at Gun Creek.

Walk around the Virgin Gorda Yacht Harbour. Take a look at all the sailboats and motor yachts.

Stop by the Mine Shaft Cafe at sunset time. You'll see one of the world's great views. Stay for a romantic, casual meal under the stars.

GREAT BOAT TRIPS AND BOAT RENTALS IN THE VALLEY

There are several great cruises available that will take you snorkeling or sight-seeing. On a calm day it's also quite easy and a lot of fun to rent a little boat and go from the Virgin Gorda Yacht Harbour to The Baths and other nearby beaches.

CAPTAINED BOAT TRIPS FROM THE VALLEY

Let someone else do the driving and sit back and enjoy the remarkable views from the water when you take one of these cruises. Choose a sail boat or a powerboat and pick a planned itinerary or create your own!

Spirit of Anegada (*496.6825, www.spiritofanegada.com*), based at the Yacht Harbour, offers daily sailing trips on a 49' sailboat, the *Spirit of Anegada*. The captain usually sails to uninhabited islands for some excellent snorkeling. A hot luncheon is served on board. The cost is $95 per person (minimum 4 people, maximum 10). The *Spirit of Anegada* is also available for half-day trips for $60 per person including beverages or for private charter to almost anywhere for $650 a day or $400 a half day, and also ask about their sunset cruise.

Euphoric Cruises (*495.5542*) has a 28' Bertram powerboat that is available for day trips with a captain. The boat leaves from Virgin Gorda Yacht Harbour and will head to your choice of island(s), weather permitting. Cost is $750 for a full day; $500 a half day. They have a 36' Riviera for $1,000 a day, $650 a half day.

Double "D" Charters (*495.6150, 499.2479*) has a great round trip to Anegada that leaves from the Virgin Gorda Yacht Harbour on Thursdays or almost any day. Their 43' cabin cruiser leaves at 9 am and returns around 5 pm. The rate is $85 per person (six person minimum). Add on an additional $35 per person for ground transportation on Anegada and a lobster lunch at the Big Bamboo on Loblolly Bay. Also check out their other cruise opportunities on their 50' sailboat and 49' catamaran.

RENTING YOUR OWN LITTLE BOAT

Power Boat Rentals, Ltd. (*495.5542*). At Virgin Gorda Yacht Harbour, Ash Harrigan offers 18' and 24' Boston Whalers, all with biminis, vhf radio, stepladder, and anchor. Rates are $200-$250 per day. Call for weekly rates. They'll deliver boats to (or pick you up in) Virgin Gorda and also Road Town and Trellis Bay in Tortola.

111

GREAT TRAILS AND NATURE STOPS IN THE VALLEY

The BVI National Parks Trust maintains many parks and protected areas throughout the BVI, including The Baths, the beaches to the north and south of The Baths, and Gorda Peak National Park. There are trails and picnic spots throughout the parks. One can do this on foot or on horseback. Virgin Gorda also has a wonderful nature center.

GORDA PEAK NATIONAL PARK

This 265-acre park sits atop the highest area of Virgin Gorda (the peak is 1359'). Both the south and north entrances are reachable from the main road between The Valley and North Sound. Signs and access are on the west side of the road. Look for a small sign at each entrance. Here you will find fairly strenuous trails, a lookout tower, and picnic tables. The dense vegetation includes stately mahogany trees and exotic, colorful orchids.

DEVIL'S BAY AND STONEY BAY

There are inland and coastal trails from The Baths to Devil's Bay, where you will find tranquil waters and good snorkeling. From Devil's Bay there is a trail that goes on to Stoney Bay.

HORSEBACK RIDING

Take a sunrise or sunset ride beside the shimmering sea, along a beautiful beach. Call Alexander Parillon (*496.4978*).

LITTLE SECRETS NATURE CENTER

Wander around inside and out at this delightful display of flora and fauna indigenous to the BVI. Come see the world's smallest lizard, soldier and hermit crabs, tortoises, iguanas, turtles, tarantulas, and scorpions all crawling around in their natural habitat. See turpentine trees, giant cotton trees, century plants, and cactus. Tall trees reach up to the skylights inside, and outside walkways and boardwalks curve around giant boulders and lead to secret grottoes showcasing such things as a giant ficus tree root and a huge termite nest. Peer into ponds for examples of aquatic plants and various fish. Slip through a crack in a rock and find yourself in a secret garden lush with local plants. Magnification displays offer big views of the tinier creatures. There's a small gift shop. If you are interested in ecological nature walks on Virgin Gorda, inquire about hiring a guide. *Drive south from the Yacht Harbour to the round-a-bout and the Rock Cafe and turn right, toward the Post Office. The Center is on your left. (495.5954.)*

GREAT SHOPPING IN THE VALLEY

Shopping in the Valley is limited but interesting. The Virgin Gorda Yacht Harbour has two little collections of shops, one on either side of the main parking lot. The BVI Tourist Board has an office here well-stocked with maps, brochures, and menus. Shops are also located at the entrance to The Baths and at Little Dix Bay Resort (see page 114).

VIRGIN GORDA YACHT HARBOUR SHOPPING

Buck's Food Market (*495.5423*) is Virgin Gorda's supermarket, and you'll find fresh, canned, and frozen foods.

Blue Banana (*495.6633*) features a great variety of beautiful and sophisticated items. Come here for scrunchies, sarongs, candles, pottery, bathing suits, jewelry, colorful cotton pants and tops, note cards, sun hats, and lovely lightweight handmade sweaters.

DIVE BVI (*495.5513*) carries great T-shirts, sunglasses, books, and sportswear as well as diving and snorkel equipment (including on-the-spot prescription masks). They also offer dives and instruction.

Kaunda's Kysy Tropix (*495.5636*) is the place to come for a great selection of music CDs—reggae, steel bands, rock, top 40s, etc. Also, you can bring your film here for quick processing. They pierce ears, too!

Margo's Jewelry Boutique (*495.5237*) showcases handcrafted gold and silver pieces of jewelry and carved wood sculptures.

Ocean Delight Ice Cream Parlour (*495.54540*), hidden behind the Wine Cellar, scoops up icy cold treats in assorted flavors.

O'Neal Drug Centre (*495.5449*) is a good source for prescriptions as well as everything from Band-Aids and shampoo to notebooks and pencils.

Thee Artistic Gallery (*495.5104*) displays 14K gold and silver jewelry, books, colorful maps, wind chimes, and watercolors by local artists.

Virgin Gorda Craft Shop (*495.5137*) is tucked back in the corner and easy to miss but be sure to stop here for wonderful locally-made items.

Wine Cellar and Bakery (*495.5250*) carries oven-fresh French bread plus pastries, sodas, wines, and bottled liquor, and, on season, sandwiches.

SHOPPING ELSEWHERE IN THE VALLEY

Caribbean Flavor #1 (*495.5914*) is located in the pastel blue gingerbread-trimmed cottage at the entrance to The Baths and built around a boulder (it sticks up out of the middle of the floor). Come here for Caribbean CDs including CDs by local entertainer Morris Mark, colorful wind chimes, candles, a large display of original handmade silver bracelets and money clips, numerous T-shirts, toe rings, books on the Caribbean, and a great choice of local artwork.

Caribbean Flavor #2 (*495.6288*), sister shop to the above, is in the row of shops on the walkway to the restaurant and is delightful and not to be missed. It's tiny but chock-full of beautiful casual dresses and resort wear: sundresses, sarongs, pull-on pants with whimsical prints, unusual little T-shirts, and much more.

Little Dix Pavilion Gift Shop (*495.5555*), at Little Dix Resort, caters to the well-heeled, and is an excellent stop for designer bathing suits, fashionable beach cover-ups, upscale men's and women's resortwear, and fancy sandals. There's also a selection of local pottery and artwork, some nice picture frames, and plenty of Little Dix logo items, from comfortable T-shirts to hats, beach towels, and bar glasses. If you are searching for a current copy of *The New York Times*, the *Wall Street Journal*, a current news magazine, or even a new paperback, head here.

A COW STORY

Those grates made of round steel bars that you occasionally drive over, such as the one at the entrance to the Virgin Gorda Yacht Harbour, are designed to keep out hoofed animals like goats and cows (the animals lose their footing on the bars).

However, cows are smart. Hang around the Yacht Harbour's parking lot for a few minutes and you are bound to see a large cow shoulder her way, effortlessly and without missing a beat, right through the people gate, as she heads toward wherever it is she is going.

THE VALLEY'S GREAT RESTAURANTS AND BARS

There are a number of excellent restaurants in Virgin Gorda's Valley area. Don't be alarmed if you are the only customer. In the U.S. this could mean the restaurant is no good. In the BVI it indicates nothing. Virgin Gorda has relatively few visitors so sometimes a reStsaurant serves very few meals in a day. The food is still excellent and the staff will be delighted you dropped by. Be sure also to check out the restaurant section for Virgin Gorda's North Sound (see page 127). If you don't want to make the drive at night you can take a taxi or you might want to head there for a wonderful lunchtime adventure.

Chez Bamboo (*495.5752*), just north of the Yacht Harbour, features a delightfully romantic garden setting: tables surrounded by lush plants, tiny twinkling lights, and tropical breezes. More tables and a tiny bar are inside, along with some interesting murals, a deep blue ceiling and sparkles. The menu is eclectic. Good appetizers include the baked brie in puff pastry, grilled portobello with polenta, and an andouille pizza, and tasty entrees include jerk pork loin, spicy barbecue shrimp, and grilled filet mignon with baby veggies. End the evening with hot apple crisp, creme brulee, or the retro pineapple upside-down cake for two. *D $$-$$$*

Dog and Dolphin Bar and Restaurant (*494.8000*), at Nail Bay, is high up the hill and shows off stunning views of sea and neighboring islands. This very casual spot is nestled against a stunning free-form swimming pool with a classy swim-up bar and surrounded by vibrantly colorful clusters of bougainvillea. Dine right at the bar or at little bistro tables open to the breezes. For dinner, the appetizer conch fritters are excellent. Then choose grilled chicken stuffed with goat cheese, pan-fried grouper filet with mustard sauce, or barbecued spare ribs. The lunch menu features burgers, hot dogs, conch fritters, sandwiches, and salads, including an excellent jerk chicken and vegetable salad. Both the vegetable and chicken rotis are outstanding. This restaurant is a bit out of the way for dinner if you are staying in the Valley but it's definitely a lovely lunchtime stop and if you dine there you can use the pool. *LD $$*

Flying Iguana (*495.5277*) is not to be missed! It overlooks the airport runway and the sea and you can watch little planes come and go. Tables are on a small porch and, although the decor may appear ultra casual, the chef pays exquisite attention to what goes on the plate. Great choices at lunch are the beautifully

115

prepared hamburger, the BLT (arranged in a pita), the outstanding lobster fritters (available as an appetizer at night), and the club sandwich. In the evening, try the Duck by Puck (he's the owner), the fisherman's catch, the curried coconut shrimp, or the local lobster. Pancakes and various egg dishes are served in the morning. *BLD $-$$*

Giorgio's Table (*495.5684*), a 10-minute drive north of Yacht Harbour on Mahoe Bay (take a left just north of Savannah Bay and prepare for a very steep drop), is a sophisticated-looking restaurant set right at the water's edge and floor-to-ceiling glass doors open and close to regulate the breezes. This is a peaceful place to come for lunch and have a pizza and a salad. For dinner, you can choose one of the many ravioli specials, other Italian dishes, or steak. Dinner, especially if you have an appetizer or soup, can be astonishingly expensive. *LD $$$*

Little Dix Resort's Pavilion Restaurant (*495.5555*) serves exceptionally fine Continental cuisine in a stunning open-air setting with a glorious view and is a terrific place to come for any meal, day or night. Dinner here is a la carte, except for the lavish Monday night buffet. Start with carpaccio of beef and lobster or the seafood Newburg. For a main course try the penne with chili peppers, basil, and olives in plum tomato sauce; the yellow fin tuna with sweet potato mash and red pepper coulis; or the roast duckling l'orange. Breakfast and lunch, which are served buffet-style but elegantly, are outstanding and definitely the best buffets in the BVI. At lunch, which is a truly relaxing experience, there is large table filled with a tempting array of composed salads, platters of imported cheeses, bowls of fresh fruits, and assorted breads. Head to the grill for excellent fresh fish, great hamburgers and hot dogs, and other hot entrees. Then linger with a sampling from the table of tempting sweets. The lunch buffet is $25 ($18 without hot items). Breakfast is $18. *Long pants and collared shirts required for men after sunset. Reservations are necessary for dinner. BLD $$$*

Mad Dog (*495.5830*) is a tiny and very casual open-air bar tucked among the sea grapes just before the parking circle for The Baths. Come here for hot dogs, BLTs, tuna sandwiches, cold beer, and their real claim to fame, frozen Pina Coladas. *Open 10 am-7 pm. L $*

Mine Shaft Cafe (*495.5260*) is a casual place perched atop a hill and shows off superb scenery. Views from the sunken bar and inside tables are awesome but the view from the deck is even better: unbelievably brilliant sunsets and at night a billion stars and the lights of Tortola twinkling across the channel! Nachos, burgers, steak sandwiches, wings, and ribs, hamburgers, rotis, and Caesar salad with grilled chicken are the house specialties. You'll find it on the road to Coppermine Point. *D $*

Rock Cafe (*495.5482*) consists of an air-conditioned indoor dining room and bar and three levels of outdoor deck exquisitely designed to wrap around giant boulders and trees. Tables are hidden here and there (one table has a private deck all to itself) and water trickles gently down a waterfall. Italian cuisine is the specialty here. Try the spaghetti with red or white clam sauce, penne alla putanesca, spaghetti with lobster, penne with chicken and brocolli, or the penne caprese (served the traditional Italian way, at room temperature). Other good choices are the fresh local fish or the strip loin with grilled herbs. Save room for the chocolate mousse, homemade and the house specialty. Stick around for entertainment late into the night at Sam's Piano Bar (*see below*). There's also a late night menu of pizzas and snacks. *D $$*

NIGHTLIFE IN THE VALLEY

There's usually something happening most nights a week but the exact schedule of who is playing where and when is in a state of constant flux. When you are on island, look for the Limin' Times *for the weekly schedule of entertainment. Also look for signs and posters pasted on telephone poles and on various walls around the Virgin Gorda Yacht Harbour, especially near the Bath and Turtle.*

The Bath and Turtle (*495.5239*) draws crowds every Wednesday night to listen and dance to live local bands.

Chez Bamboo (*495.5752*) features a live band on Fridays.

Flying Iguana (*495.5277*) is the locale for the popular band Profile on Tuesday evenings.

Little Dix Resort (*495.5555*) on season, has entertainment every evening but Sunday.

Mine Shaft Cafe and Nightclub (*495.5260*) is the place to come for great full-moon parties.

Sam's Piano Bar at the Rock Cafe (*495.5482*) is the hottest nightspot on Virgin Gorda. Six nights a week European pianist Carl Williams delights the crowds with music and song that spans the decades, from swanky Frank to Billy Joel to renditions of the latest hits. Take a seat around the piano bar or settle into the 1950s-style chairs or chill out in a cozy alcove in this large and dimly lit and hugely appealing nightclub. *8 pm-midnight Sun.-Tues. and also Thurs.-Fri. (closed Wed.); 8 pm-2 am Sat.*

THE VALLEY'S GREAT RESORTS AND VILLAS

In the Valley on Virgin Gorda you can choose a luxury resort, an intimate inn, comfortable cottages, or a fancy villa. Few places have rooms keys but you can lock yourself in at night, if you wish. To check out the resorts on Virgin Gorda's North Sound, see page 130.

Rates are per night for two people on season (off-season in parentheses), without meals and without 7% government tax and 10%-12% service charge.

GUAVABERRY SPRING BAY VACATION HOMES
When you want the comfort of having a kitchen, whether you want a simple cottage or an ultra-fancy villa with a pool, check into charming Guavaberry.

Guavaberry's cottages and villas are about a mile-and-a-half south of Yacht Harbor and just north of The Baths and are on or within walking distance of lovely Spring Bay Beach. All units are fully equipped and the living is easy here. The hexagonal wooden cottages are scattered in the hills and hover at treetop level, many with great views of neighboring islands. These simple one- and two-bedroom units have separate living/dining areas, compact but complete kitchens, and comfortable decks. The cottages are beautifully positioned to capture the breezes and one wakes to a songbird serenade.

The wonderful collection of private villas, ranging in size from a studio to five bedrooms, offers something for everyone. All have views, whether right on the beach, or built into the boulders, or poking out of tropical greenery. Kitchens are fully equipped, right down to the little details, like garlic presses. Some villas have stunning private swimming pools and some have air-conditioned bedrooms. One has a tennis court. All are comfortably and stylishly furnished and some are extremely elegant.

Daily maid service is provided for both cottages and villas. A delightfully well-stocked little commissary carries everything from peanut butter to frozen spinach to rental snorkel equipment to beer, wine, and champagne. If you want fresh bread put your order in by 3 pm. There are safes in all units, no TVs, and phones in the villas only. Management is truly outstanding.
18 cottages, 16 villas. Rates (plus 7% tax but no additional service charge): one-bedroom cottage $185 ($120), two-bedroom cottage $265 ($175); villas $1,850 ($1,274) to $7,620 ($4,950) per week. No credit cards. General Manager: Tina Goschler. Tel: 284.495.5227. Fax: 284.495.5283. P.O. Box 20. Web: www.guavaberryspringbay.com

118

KATITCHE POINT GREATHOUSE

For a luxurious splurge for up to 10 people (or just the two of you), rent this fabulous villa out on a point with spectacular views of water and distant islands.

Five exquisitely-decorated suites, a stunning disappearing-edge pool, a Viking kitchen, a wide-screen TV, Bose sound, breakfast prepared for you, a path down to the beach and snorkeling...what more could you want?
Weekly rates: 5 suites $16,445 ($14,548); 4 suites $13,018 ($11,120); Just the two of you $5,000 plus 12% service charge. Reservations: 284.495.5672 or rentals@katitchepoint.de. Web: www.katitchepoint.com

LITTLE DIX BAY

This luxury resort, a Rosewood property, runs along the crescent-shaped shore of one of Virgin Gorda's calmest and prettiest bays.

Little Dix Bay is an upscale, elegant retreat just north of town. It's quiet and peaceful here. Despite the fact that this is one of the largest resorts in the BVI, you can feel wonderfully alone. Rooms, all with patios or balconies, are two or four to a building and scattered over a half-mile of beautifully-manicured grounds. Some have great views, and some are hidden among the trees, but all are spacious and handsomely furnished. King beds back up to stunning stone walls, beams run across the ceilings, and bathrooms are roomy with walk-in showers big enough for two. All units are air-conditioned. One-bedroom suites have a soaking tub and two- and three-bedroom villas have private pools. A luxurious spa sits on the hillside, with a curvy two-tier plunge pool, nine treatment cottages (including one roomy enough for two guests to be treated together) built to allow treatments in air-conditioned comfort or outside in soft breezes with sea views, and a fantastic menu of spa services.

The Pavilion Restaurant (*see page 116*), an open-air affair with an absolutely stunning view, is the setting for lavish buffet breakfasts and lunches and quiet and elegant a la carte dinners. The intimate Sugar Mill restaurant, al fresco and open on season, is nestled behind the inviting stone-walled bar. The casual Beach Grill serves sandwiches, salads, and grilled fish and steaks for lunch and dinner. Head to the long silken beach for a peaceful walk, find yourself a float and relax or look for turtles, snorkel (it's best at the northern edge of the beach), hike to Savannah Bay (just when you are sure you're lost in the woods, you'll suddenly be there), play tennis (there are seven courts), or have Little Dix drop you at a deserted beach with an elegant picnic. There is a superb children's program. Men's evening dress code is collared shirt, slacks, and no sandals.
97 units. General Manager: David Flack. Rates: $450-$875 ($275-$550) plus 10% service charge. Suites and villas more. Reservations: 800.928.3000. Tel: 284.495.5555. Fax 284.495.5661. P.O. Box 70. Web: www.littledixbay.com

MAHOE BAY VILLAS
Stunning villas, each with its own private pool, face lovely Mahoe Bay.

Nestled between hillside and beach is this wonderful collection of upscale villas. Each one has a private swiming pool and there is a communal tennis court. Villas have from two to five bedrooms, are privately owned and individually furnished, and many can be rented through Virgin Gorda Villa Rentals. *17 villas. Weekly rates: $3,927-$9,044 ($2,856-$7,497) including tax and service charge (higher holidays). Tel: 284.495.7421. Fax: 284.495.7367. P.O. Box 63. Web: www.virgingordabvi.com*

NAIL BAY RESORT
Stay in a room or a suite or splurge on a fabulous villa right on the beach or up in the hills at this state-of-the-art resort and villa complex.

The dream of visionary Agit George, Nail Bay Resort is built on 147 acres of steep hillside that sweeps down to three long and slender beaches. It's on the west side of Virgin Gorda, about five miles north of the Valley. Guests rent either condo-like units or privately owned villas that range from comfortably luxurious to breathtakingly fabulous. If you fall in love with Nail Bay, as many do, you can buy land and build your own. Rooms, suites, and apartments are in two adjacent, pastel, West Indian-style frame buildings set on the hillside and looking out over the pool and restaurant to stunning views of the sea and neighboring islands. All have air-conditioning, TV/VCRs, and ultra-modern kitchenettes or kitchens. The one- to five-bedroom villas, which must conform to exacting standards concerning amenities (including cappucino machines, data ports, and DVD players) are otherwise entirely original and each is a masterpiece all its own. You'll find stunning "disappearing edge" swimming pools, windows that turn into waterfalls, private plunge pools, magnificently handcrafted stone walls, artistic sculptures and sculptured gardens, furturistic kitchens. All have fabulous views and many are air-conditioned. Hike the hills, walk the beaches, snorkel, play tennis or bocce or croquet or horseshoes, or laze in the hillside free-form pool, complete with waterfall and swim-up bar. If you don't want to cook, try In-Villa Dining or the Dog and Dolphin (*see page 115*). *35 rooms and suites, 10 villas. Rates: rooms $125-$180 ($99-$120), suites $195-$600 ($135-$375), villas $270-$900 ($160-$525) plus 10% service charge. General Manager: Monica Ramgeet. Tel: 800.871.3551 or 284.495.5452. Fax 284.495.5875. P.O. Box 69. Web: www.nailbay.com*

OLDE YARD VILLAGE
The Olde Yard Inn has closed and appealing condos are being built on the site. To buy or rent, call Carol or Jill Kaufman (*Tel: 284.495.5544; Web: www.oldeyardvillage.com*).

PART 2: NORTH SOUND

Note: This chapter on Virgin Gorda is divided into two sections: North Sound, which begins here, and The Valley, which begins on page 105.

WHAT YOU CAN DO IN NORTH SOUND

You can stay in an elegant resort or a yachting resort or a simple hotel or you can rent a villa. North Sound is "paradise found" for water lovers. This water wonderland is the place to come for almost every possible kind of water sport. Here you can snorkel, swim, sail, windsurf, rent motorboats, and water-ski, or you can learn how to do any of these things. There are also bars, casual eateries, and an elegant restaurant.

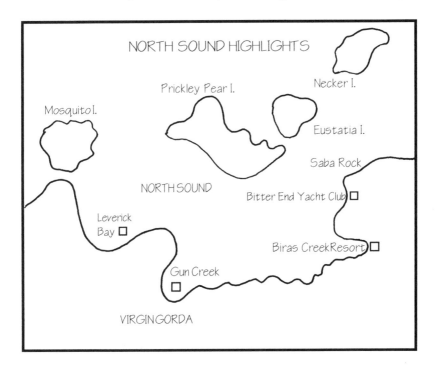

GETTING TO NORTH SOUND FROM TORTOLA OR THE VALLEY

To get here from Tortola you can take the North Sound Express from Beef Island at the east end of Tortola. It stops at Leverick Bay and Bitter End (*see Appendix for ferry schedules on page 139*). From the Valley, you can drive or take a taxi to Leverick Bay or Gun Creek.

121

EXPLORING NORTH SOUND

In North Sound you travel mainly by water and you can take water taxis and ferries to restaurants and beaches. You can also rent your own dinghy and travel to a number of different beaches and unbelievably great snorkeling spots.

Hiring a Water Taxi

You can hire a water taxi at the **Water Sports Center at Leverick Bay** (*495.7366*) to take you to Bitter End. The taxi will pick you up at Bitter End for the trip back any time you want before 5 pm. Round trip fare is $25.

Taking a Little Ferry

Free ferries (*see schedule, page 140*) run between Gun Creek and The Bitter End Yacht Club, and there are many boat trips that leave from The Bitter End (*see page 124*). If you want to dine at Saba Rock, call 495.7711 and a ferry will come and pick you up at any other North Sound dock (Leverick Bay, Gun Creek, Biras Creek, Bitter End).

Renting a Dinghy or a Powerboat

The Bitter End Yacht Club (*494.2746*) rents Boston Whalers starting at $50 a half-day. At **Leverick Bay**, the **Water Sports Center** (*495.7376*) rents 10' dinghies with 10 hp engines. Rates start at $60 a half-day, $75 a full day. If you want something larger, get the 24' center console powerboat with bimini for $280 a day plus fuel.

EXPLORING NORTH SOUND BY DINGHY

North Sound is an absolutely wonderful place to explore in a dinghy. There are deserted beaches to visit and great snorkeling spots to anchor near. There is very calm water to drift about in and restaurants and bars to motor over to. For a quiet ride, putter in towards Deep Bay or around the outskirts of Eustatia Sound. Be very careful and go very slowly near Eustatia Sound Reef. The water gets pretty shallow and you don't want to run over and damage any coral. When you feel like lunch or a snack or a beverage, just tie your boat up at the dinghy docks at Saba Rock or the Bitter End Yacht Club or Leverick Bay or the Fat Virgin at Biras Creek or the Sand Box on Prickly Pear. Be sure to bring and use sunscreen (it can be so breezy and cool on the water that it is hard to remember that the sun can still burn).

BEACHES AND WATER SPORTS ON NORTH SOUND

There are some nice beaches on North Sound and really great snorkeling spots are practically everywhere. To rent watersports equipment, head to Leverick Bay or The Bitter End Yacht Club.

Beaches

The best beaches are reachable by dinghy. Head to Vixen Point on Prickly Pear for a lovely point of soft white sand and very calm water. The Sand Box restaurant is here. About midway on the west side of Prickly Pear is Honeymoon Beach, a tiny beach that's just about the right size for two. Around to the north (take the passage between Prickly Pear and Saba Rock and then bear west) is a long stretch of beach, which is a lovely stop on a calm day but beware there is no shade. You can dinghy over to the west side of Eustatia Island for a small beach with a nice view of Necker Island or head to the east side of the island to the long beach that looks across to Bitter End. Bitter End has a narrow beach.

Sailboards, Kayaks, Alden Rowing Shells, and Sail Boats

The Bitter End Yacht Club (*494.2746*) has a huge variety of water sports rentals. Come here to rent sailboards, sunfish, lasers, 19' Rhodes, J-24 sailboats, kayaks, Alden Rowing Shells, and more. Rates are $15-$20 per hour. **The Water Sports Center** at Leverick Bay (*495.7376*) rents sunfish, Hobi Waves, and kayaks. Instruction is available in water-skiing, sunfishing, and Hobie Cat sailing for no additional charge.

Parasailing and Water-skiing

The Water Sports Center (*495.7376*) at Leverick Bay is the place to come for a thrilling parasailing ride for people age 2 to 92! You'll spot turtles and sea rays from 600' up. Rates are $55 for 10 minutes. Water-ski off of their competition mastercraft ski boat. Rates are $90 an hour, $60 a half hour. Barefooters use the barefoot bom and wakeboarders try the skylon pylon.

Snorkeling

Head to the reefs all around Eustatia Sound, the reefs on the east and west sides of Eustatia Island, Cactus Reef just off the northwest end of Prickly Pear Island, Honeymoon Beach, Little Trunk Bay south of Mosquito Island, and the windward side of Prickly Pear Island. If you need snorkel equipment, rent it from **The Water Sports Center** (*495.7376*) at Leverick Bay for $8 a day or buy it at DIVE BVI (*495.7328*).

123

GREAT CAPTAINED BOAT AND SNORKELING TRIPS FROM NORTH SOUND

Statia Reef Snorkel Trip
Join one of the twice-daily snorkel trips to beautiful Statia Reef on the 40' Ponce de Leon, a boat specially designed for snorkeling. The short morning trip, which makes one stop, is $5 per person. In the afternoon, there are three snorkeling stops for $10 per person. Call The Bitter End (*494.2746*).

Night Snorkeling
Take a guided night-snorkeling tour of Statia Reef led by the famous Kilbride group. Call The Bitter End (*494.2746*). This is offered in the summer only.

Powerboat to Anegada
Ride in comfort on the diesel-powered Corinthian to Anegada. On Tuesdays you get a chance to explore the island, go to the beach, snorkel, and have lunch at the Big Bamboo. The boat leaves at 9:30 and returns about 5:30. The fare is $60 per person, including lunch. Call The Bitter End (*494.2746*).

Cigarette boat to Anegada or around the BVI
The **Water Sports Center at Leverick Bay** (*495.7376*) usually offers full-day trips to Anegada. You go to Loblolly Bay or Cow Wreck Beach. The cost is $650 (8 person maximum).

Starlight Cruise
Cruise around North Sound under the stars while sipping champagne. The boat leaves at 6 pm and returns about 7:30 pm, sometimes with a steel band. Cost is $30 per person. Make reservations with The Bitter End (*494.2746*).

Ultimate Beaches
Sit back and relax and let a captain take you to one of many secluded beaches on a 26' speedboat. Or go to them all! It's your choice. Rates for two people are $400 per day, $225 a half-day. Call The Bitter End Yacht Club (*494.2746*).

Deep-Sea Fishing
The **Bitter End** (*494.2746*) runs half-day offshore fishing trips on a 26' speedboat. Rates are $450 per day and $275 for a half-day. **Virgin Gorda Charter Services** (*495.6666*) offers half-day and full-day deep-sea fishing charters. Catch wahoo, tuna, swordfish, and more.

124

Sailing to Other Islands

Spice (*495.7044*), or book through Leverick Bay Watersports (*495.7376*), combines great snorkeling with outstanding sailing. This 51' sloop is perfect for a full or half-day of exploring the BVI waters. Cruise to the Baths, Cooper Island, the Dogs, Norman Island, Anegada, or even Jost Van Dyke. Experience extraordinary snorkeling and visit cool little beach bars. Every Thursday the *Spice* heads to Anegada for the day. Full days are $85 and half days are $55 per person. A private charter is $600 (maximum of 8).

Trip to Norman Island

Take this trip down the Sir Francis Drake Channel and snorkel at the famous Caves. The boat leaves every Thursday at 9:30 am and the cost, including a barbecue lunch, is $60 per person. Call The Bitter End Yacht Club (*494.2746*).

SNORKEL TRIPS

DIVE BVI (*495.7328*) takes snorkerlers on their afternoon dives. Call to find out where the dive boats are going on a particular day.

SHOPPING IN NORTH SOUND

LEVERICK BAY SHOPPING

Chef's Pantry at Leverick Bay (*495.7154*) carries groceries, fresh produce, liquor and beer, canned goods, frozen meats, cheeses, and snacks.

DIVE BVI (*495.7328*) sells a variety of swimwear, hats, postcards, colorful T-shirts, collared shirts in bright designs, local artwork including Flukes prints, and island books, and rents and sells snorkel and diving gear.

Palm Tree Gallery (*495.7479*) is definitely worth a stop (it's in the back of the plaza, past DIVE BVI). There are many wonderful things to buy here. Look at the lovely selection of jewelry including fish, sea shell, and sailboat charms. This is also the place to come for handmade Caribbean batik, art from the BVI and other Caribbean islands, island books, postcards, wind chimes, candles, and appealing decorative boxes.

Pusser's Company Store (*495.7369*) carries a large collection of fashionable but comfortable clothing for the whole family, plus all sizes of bottles of their famous rum, as well as souvenirs, postcards, and books.

NORTH SOUND RESORT SHOPPING

Fat Virgin's Treasure (*495.7054*) is at the Biras Creek Resort, right behind the Fat Virgin Cafe. Tie up your dinghy at the dock and spend some time here. You'll find fashionable sunglasses, colorful hats, bathing suits, chic resortwear, local art and pottery, frameable maps, delightful pottery, island books, and many items marked with the well-known Biras Creek Resort logo.

Bitter End Emporium (*495.2746*) features freshly baked breads and pastries, gourmet items, and canned goods, plus slices of pizza.

Saba Rock Resort Gift Shop (*495.7711*) is an elegant stop. Dark wood paneled walls and air-conditioning provide a respite from the sun. Browse through neat piles of men's and women's shorts, pants, and shirts; shelves of books; plus watches, sunglasses, and nautical items.

THE SPA AT LEVERICK BAY

When you're in the mood for a bit of extra-special pampering make an appointment here for all types of massages, body wraps and treatments, and facials. *495.7375*

NORTH SOUND'S GREAT RESTAURANTS AND BARS

All of these places are easily reachable by dinghy if you are already in North Sound. If you happen to be coming from the Valley, you can drive directly to the Restaurant at Leverick Bay. For the rest, you will need to catch a ferry (see Appendix for schedules on page 140) *or arrrive by dinghy. Some restaurants will send a boat for you free of charge* (see individual restaurant descriptions).

Biras Creek Resort (*494.3555*) has one of the most romantic dining rooms in the Caribbean. It's in the "Castle," a stunning stonework structure set on top of a hill and overlooking both the Caribbean Sea and the calm North Sound. The expansive terrace and al fresco lounge are breathtaking settings for an evening cocktail. Come here to catch the ever-changing colors of the sky at sunset and, after dark, watch the twinkling lights on the distant hillsides compete with the stars. Dinner is elegant and served by candlelight in several open-air dining rooms. The sophisticated four-course menu changes nightly and always includes a number of choices for appetizers, main courses, and desserts. Starters might include cream of sweet potato soup, polenta-crusted oysters, Caesar salad and five-spice duck salad. Entrees could be grilled mahi mahi with a chorizo rissotto, grilled loin of veal with spinach and a cream of root vegetables, honey-roasted duck breast, and a filet mignon with Bernaise sauce. Lobster (for a surcharge) and a vegetarian dish are always offered. Dessert choices might be a chocolate tart with warm chocolate sauce, banana creme brulee, or white chocolate mousse with a mango-lime salsa. The cuisine and service here are outstanding and the setting is truly one of the very best in the BVI. This is a spot to have a splendid dinner, and then linger over Biras Creek's signature fourth-course offering of port and Stilton. The wine list here is exceptional. The prix fixe dinner is $65 per person plus 15% service. Biras Creek will provide complimentary boat transportation from Gun Creek or Bitter End. *Dress is casual elegant (long trousers and collared shirts for men). Reservations for dinner and transportation essential. D $$$*

The Clubhouse at **The Bitter End Yacht Club** (*494.2746*) offers casual meals in an open-air dining room. Breakfast, for $17.50, includes a buffet plus a choice of eggs, pancakes, or French toast. Lunch is $19 and includes a buffet of salads, plus a choice of entrees such as a hamburger, chef salad, or conch fritters. Dinner, for $38, includes a salad and dessert buffet plus a choice of entrees such as ribs, steaks, fish, or lobster (for a surcharge). *BLD $$-$$$*

127

Fat Virgin's Cafe (*495.7052*), at Biras Creek Marina Village and reachable by dinghy, is very casual and prepares superb sandwiches and salads all day long. Come here for a great hamburger, a terrific chicken or vegetable roti, and an outstanding tuna salad sandwich on a five-grain bread. The menu is the same day and night, except on Friday, when you can also get a full selection of Chinese offerings. *LD (closes 6 pm off-season) $$*

Last Stop Bar (*no phone*), up a little incline just across from the Gun Creek dock and overlooking the water, is a tiny little bar that serves beverages all day long. This is a good stop when you are waiting for a ferry or a taxi. *$*

Restaurant at Leverick Bay (*495.7154*), at Leverick Bay, is actually two places. The courtyard is the place to come for a delicious lobster salad or a traditional club sandwich, or a BLT, plus burgers, and pizzas. Breakfast is served here, too. Upstairs and open to the breezes you'll find a small lounge area and long rectangular bar, plus tables overlooking the water. Good choices for starters are the sweet potato soup and the grilled scallop and parma ham skewers. Then move on to the grilled local swordfish, Anegada lobster, pan-seared filet mignon with Bernaise sauce, or ossobuco. Look for the blackboard of nightly specials. *BLD $$*

Sand Box (*495.9122*), a barefoot beach bar at Vixen Point on Prickly Pear Island, is the place to come for burgers, salads, and sandwiches at lunch and conch chowder, pumpkin soup, grilled sirloin steak, sauteed conch, and swordfish with a spicy Creole sauce for dinner. *Closed days when a small cruise ship is in and closed Aug. and Sept. LD $-$$*

Sharky's Pub at Saba Rock (*495.7711*) is on a rock just 200 yards or so from the Bitter End and it's a breezy, waterfront magnet for the yachting crowd who come for chicken tacos, burgers, sandwiches, and salads at lunch and return for the giant dinner buffet and salad bar for $25 or the fresh fish and salad bar combo for slightly more. Call for free pick up at any North Sound dock. *LD $-$$*

> **"There is nothing which has yet been contrived by man by which so much happiness is produced as by a good tavern or inn"**
> **— or a BVI restaurant or bar.**
>
> *— logical update of*
> *Dr. Johnson's oft-quoted comment*

NIGHTLIFE ON NORTH SOUND

Schedules change all the time so check local papers or look for a copy of the Limin' Times, *which comes out weekly and is very accurate. It's also a good idea to call before you go.*

Biras Creek Resort (*494.3555*) presents Calypso singer Mark Morris Tuesday nights, Dennis Brown and his light dancing music Thursday nights, and a great steel band every Saturday night.

Bitter End Yacht Club (*494.2746*) gets the crowds on Fridays when local bands entertain.

Restaurant at Leverick Bay (*495.7154*) features the sounds of Mark Morris Saturday nights.

Sand Box (*495.9122*) is an easy hop from The Bitter End Yacht Club or Biras Creek. Tie up at the little dingy dock. Local bands entertain Mondays and Wednesdays in season. *Closed Aug. to mid-Oct.*

Sharky's Pub at Saba Rock (*495.7711*) sits just 100 yards or so from their water taxi stand at Bitter End Yacht Club. This rock rocks nightly starting at 8 pm. Steel bands play Sunday through Thursday. Other local bands take over on the weekend nights.

BIRAS CREEK: A GREAT PLACE FOR PEACEFUL COCKTAILS

When you are looking for that "perfect" setting for a quiet cocktail, nothing beats the "Castle" terrace at **Biras Creek Resort** (*494.3555*). It's spectacularly romantic. Although distant islands hide the sun as it slips into the sea, you are high enough to catch the ever-changing colors across the enormous panorama of water, sky, and hills as you gaze across North Sound, watching the sunlight change to nightlight.

NORTH SOUND'S GREAT RESORTS AND VILLAS

Along the shores of Virgin Gorda's North Sound are several great places to stay. Three are accessible only by boat. Few places have room keys but you can lock yourself in at night, if you wish. If you want to check out the resorts in the Valley on Virgin Gorda, see page 118.

Rates are per night for two people on season (off-season in parentheses), without meals (unless otherwise stated), and without 7% tax and 10% or 12% service.

BIRAS CREEK RESORT

One of the Caribbean's most romantic and intimate hideaways, and one of only five Relais & Chateaux in the Caribbean, this is a sophisticated escape, a place to come for superb cuisine, sparkling service, and elegant, comfortable suites.

Biras Creek is spread out over 140 acres on a peninsula and is accessible only by boat. Suites are in duplex cottages, most of which are tucked here and there along the water's edge. All have very private entrances that are hidden among tropical flowers so you never know you are sharing a building with someone else. These spacious and inviting suites include a comfortable sitting area with a coffee maker and little fridge, a separate bedroom, a delightful garden shower open to the sky, a CD player, safe, bikes, and a large and very private patio. The two Grand Suites are outstanding romantic retreats, each with a large and extremely comfortable living room with a veranda, a giant bedroom with its own veranda, and a spacious bathroom with an outdoor shower for two and a soaking tub with a fabulous view. Dinner (*see page 127*) and drinks are served in the "Castle," a splendid stonework structure set high on a hill with knock-out views of both the surfy Caribbean sea and tranquil North Sound. Guests gather in the open-air lounge and on the terrace for before-dinner drinks and after-dinner, three nights a week, to dance romantically under the stars. Sail-A-Way packages include two nights on a captained private yacht.

This is an incredibly easy place to do nothing or anything. Head to the secluded swimming beach or the spectacular pool overlooking the ocean, explore North Sound in a dinghy, play tennis or snooker, ride a bike, hike, be dropped at a deserted beach with a picnic, take a sail to Anegada. Before bed, relax on your patio—the total absence of artificial light makes for extraordinary stargazing. *33 suites. Rates (including meals, use of dinghies, 26' Folk sailing boats, escorted snorkel trips, much more): $750-$850 ($525-$625); Grand Suites $1,050 ($825); 2 bedroom Suite $1,650 ($1,125) plus 10% service charge. General Managers: Michael and Luciana Nijdam. Reservations: 800.223.1108. Tel: 284.494.3555. Fax: 284.494.3557. P.O. Box 54. Web: www.biras.com.*

BITTER END YACHT CLUB
Practically a scheduled stop for charterers (if it's Thursday this must be the Bitter End), this busy marina cum resort is a great spot for families and couples who like sailing or who want to learn how.

Accessible only by water, the Bitter End Yacht Club is nestled along the shore overlooking North Sound and Statia Sound and has 100 moorings. The waterfront area is bustling, with boaters coming ashore for provisions, kids taking sailing lessons, couples heading out on dinghies. Beachfront Villas (which are actually built low on a hill overlooking Statia Sound) are cooled by ceiling fans and are very "island-like" with floor-to-ceiling sliding glass doors on two sides, stone walls, and a wide deck, complete with hammock. The air-conditioned North Sound Suites are high on a hill above the pool and look out to the west across North Sound. The beaches aren't top-notch here but you can dingy to several wonderful ones and there's great snorkeling all over the place. There's also a pool (usually closed September), a fitness trail, and hiking trails.

The real draw here is sailing and learning how to sail. Guests have unlimited use of the resort's outstanding fleet of over 100 day boats, including Hobie waves, Vanguard 15s, Sunfish, Escapes, Optimists, Lasers, Rhodes 19s, J-24s, Mistral Windsurfers, Rowing sculls, Boston Whaler tenders, and ocean kayaks. If you need instruction, just ask one of the water sports staff. The popular Admiral's Package includes all meals, an introductory sailing course (The Nick Trotter Sailing School is located here), daily excursions to other islands and snorkeling trips, and unlimited use of the BEYC fleet. You can also stay overnight on a 30' sailboat even if you have never been on a boat before.
95 units, including 8 "Freedom 30" Yachts. FAP Rates: $585-850 ($430-$525); Admiral's Package rates for 7 nights: $4,095-$5,950 ($3,010-$3,675), plus 11% service charge. General Manager: Ross Justice. Reservations: 800.872.2392. Tel: 284.494.2746. Fax 284.494.4756. P.O. Box 46. Web: www.beyc.com

EUSTATIA ISLAND RETREAT
For a pampering escape, complete with gourmet chef, rent this island retreat.

Just north of Virgin Gorda and bordering North Sound is privately-owned 22-acre Eustatia Island. Two spacious villas with handsome stone walls and rooms open to the breezes are nestled against the rocky shore on the leeward side of the island and can accommodate up to 10 people. At your beck and call is a staff and chef and out your front door are all the delights North Sound has to offer.
Daily Rates $4,500 up to 6 people, $6,570 7-10 people plus 8% service charge (off-season less). Solaris Management. Tel: 284.495.9411. Fax 284.495.9410. P.O. Box 62. Web: www.eustatiabvi.com

131

LEVERICK BAY RESORT
The small hillside hotel here is a perfect economical stop if you like water sports and want to spend your days exploring North Sound.

Leverick Bay, although tiny, is the largest "settlement" at the north end of Virgin Gorda and consists of a marina, restaurant, day spa, and a cluster of shops. Simple but nicely decorated hotel rooms run along a hillside and the views are terrific from the rooms and balconies. There are also suites with full kitchens. You can watch the activity at the little dock down below or rent a dinghy, catch a day sail, water-ski, or parasail. There's a tiny sliver of beach and a small pool. *14 rooms. Rates $149 (off-season $119); suites more. General Manager: Monica Willis. Reservations: 800.848.7081. Tel: 284.495.7421. Fax 284.495.7367. P.O. Box 63. Web: www.leverickbay.com*

SABA ROCK RESORT
There's no beach here, but you can dinghy to one, the rooms are comfortable and contemporary, and great snorkeling is everywhere.

This could be the tiniest resort property in the Caribbean. It's built on what was once just a spit of a rock, 200 yards or so from the Bitter End Yacht Club. In fact long-time visitors to the BVI who used to pull their dinghy up to that rickety little dock and bar on the original Saba Rock will not believe their eyes. What was once barely a bar is now an eight-room resort with a large gift shop plus a popular restaurant and watering hole. The large, open-air restaurant and bar stretches along the entire south side of the islet. Rooms and two-bedrooms suites are above and one room is by itself on the north side of the islet. All are surprisingly spacious and very contemporary, with cathedral ceilings, attractive fabrics and furnishings, air-conditioning and ceiling fans, dish TV, and small balconies. Instead of a beach, there is a large sandy area with lounge chairs and hammocks and a path through beautifully manicured gardens. You can rent dinghies and take the free ferry to the Bitter End Yacht Club. *8 units. Rates $150-$350 ($125-$200). Closed Sept. General Manager: David Brick. Tel: 284.495.7711. Fax 284.495.7373. P.O. Box 540. Web: www.sabarock.com*

VIRGIN GORDA VILLA RENTALS
Choose a simple cottage or a fancy house overlooking North Sound.

Leverick Bay is the only place on North Sound with a large number of rental villas. They range in size from one to five bedrooms and some have pools. *29 villas. Weekly rates: $833-$6,545 ($714-$4,165) including tax and service charge (higher holidays). Tel: 284.495.7421. Fax: 284.495.7367. P.O. Box 63. Web: www.virgingordabvi.com*

MORE
DRIVING HINTS

ROUND-A-BOUTS

Round-a-bouts are places where four or five roads run into a circle. The driver enters the circle, drives along part of it, and then exits on the road of choice. The only people who go full circle are those who want to go back the way they came or those who've spent their lives going around in circles. Remember to turn left into the circle, and left out of the circle. And to drive clockwise when you are in the circle.

BEWARE THE MULE

There is sometimes a mule tied to a tree on the dirt road that lies between BVI Boardsailing and De Loose Mongoose on Tortola's Trellis Bay. On occasion, he tangles his rope around the trees on one side of the road and then heads over to the other side of the road to munch on tree leaves. Sometimes the rope becomes tightly stretched across the road about three feet above the ground, successfully halting all traffic. If this happens to you and you happen to be the only car in sight, hop out of whatever side of the car he's not on (mules have big teeth and like to bite) and give the rope a good tug. You should be able to get enough slack to get the rope to the ground so you can drive across it. Or you can head back to De Loose Mongoose and have another beer.

ROAD SIGNS

Although road signs have been posted in town and around the island, they are almost as unfamiliar to the residents as they are to you. For years, locals have used landmarks for directions so it really helps to know that in Road Town on Tortola everything is near the round-a-bout or Bobby's supermarket and around Tortola places are always near a bay (Sea Cow's or Long or Apple and so on).

PRACTICAL INFORMATION

ANTS

Yes, ants. The BVI has tiny, tiny little ants that can appear in a millisecond around anything they consider food, including toothpaste. Bring little baggies.

BANKING

On Tortola, you'll find banks in Road Town, including Barclay's, FirstBank Virgin Islands, Banco Popular, and Scotiabank. No other islands in the BVI have banks but there is a Barclays ATM machine in the Valley on Virgin Gorda. Tortola banks have ATM machines and there is also an ATM machine at Soper's Hole. BVI ATMs are often on the blink. Don't count on getting cash from them.

CAR RENTALS

Cars can be rented on Anegada (*see page 19*), Jost Van Dyke (*see page 35*), Tortola (*see page 65*), and Virgin Gorda (*see page 106*) and run about $60 a day. If you are staying at a resort, you will probably find it easier to get there first and then rent a car. Virtually all car rental agencies will pick you up and some resorts have rental agencies on the premises. Some roads are rugged so always be sure that your rental car has a spare tire, jack, and tire-changing tools.

CRIME

It's rare on Tortola, and exceedingly rare on the other British Virgin Islands. However, there's no point in creating temptation, so don't leave your wallet or your expensive camera lying around and lock doors on Tortola.

CURRENCY, CREDIT CARDS, AND TIPPING

The currency is the U.S. dollar. Most places take credit cards but you will encounter some establishments that take only cash, so bring some cash or traveler's checks. Also, some establishments refuse to take American Express so be sure to bring a MasterCard or Visa. There is no sales tax but there is a 7% hotel tax and hotels add a 10-13% service charge. Restaurants vary, and if no service is added, tip as you would in the States (15%-20%); if 10% service is added, then make up the difference to get to 15%-20%; if 15% service is added, only add more if you want to. Most restaurants clearly state on the menu and the bill whether or not they include a service charge. If you are at all unsure, just ask.

DOCUMENTS

U.S. citizens must have either a valid passport to enter the BVI or an original birth certificate with raised seal plus current picture ID. Definitely bring a valid passport if you can. You will find it far easier to enter the BVI and to get back into the U.S. with a valid passport.

TRAVELING TO AND FROM THE BVI
Getting to and from the BVI
American flies direct from many U.S. cities to San Juan, and connects with American Eagle flights to the little Tortola/Beef Island Airport. Delta and Continental offer a few connections through San Juan and also St. Thomas. If you are coming from the U.K., the best connection is British Airways to Antigua and then LIAT to Beef. If you are connecting to American Eagle in San Juan, it is important that you get to your American Eagle gate early, because at the gate you will get onto a bus and be taken out to your plane. When you book a flight to the BVI you will almost always be routed through San Juan, with a connecting flight to the BVI. However, if you live close to a city with nonstop service to St. Thomas and you are heading to Tortola, it can be a much more pleasant trip to fly nonstop to St. Thomas and take a ferry to Tortola, providing the plane arrival and ferry departure times match and you don't have a zillion pieces of luggage (*call Smith's Ferry 340.775.7292 or Native Son 340.774.8685 for schedules*). Ferries to Tortola depart from Charlotte Amalie, five minutes from the airport. (At East End, 30 minutes from the airport, ferries also leave for Tortola and for Jost Van Dyke). If you do this, you must tell the airport taxi coordinator that you are trying to catch a ferry and he will speed you into a taxi.

Entering the BVI
You will clear immigration and customs at the airport, or West End, or Road Town. Keep the little piece of paper they stick in your passport. It's to be collected when you leave the BVI (but don't panic if you lose it). Don't bring drugs into the BVI. This is a serious offense.

Exiting the BVI
Save some money for your return. There is a $10 per person departure tax at the airport; you pay at the separate window to the right of check in. (The fee is $5 if you are leaving by boat). If you fly to San Juan, this is where you will clear customs into the U.S. Be prepared for one of the world's longest airport walks. When you finally get to the escalators down, you will see elevators also, which are quicker if it is crowded. If you fly from the BVI to St. Thomas, this is where you will clear. After you check your baggage you collect it again to go through customs. If you take a ferry from the BVI to St. Thomas you will clear at either St. John or St. Thomas and then clear again at the St. Thomas airport. Allow plenty of time for St. Thomas airport clearance.

Luggage
The easiest thing to do, of course, is check it all the way through. If you do this, bring a carry-on with your bathing suit and whatever else you might need for one night because a small amount of luggage ends up somewhere else and it won't get back to you for a day. If you want to be extra safe, check your luggage

135

only to San Juan (or St. Thomas) and recheck it for your flight to the BVI. You'll have a better chance of getting it.

You Must Reconfirm Your Flight
Call American Airlines at their local number: 495.2559; for Continental: 1-800.231.0856; for Delta: 1-800.221.1212.

LODGING
Be prepared that even the fanciest lodging in the BVI may not provide service, cuisine, and amenities comparable to a full-service, luxury stateside resort. This is not a complaint, but rather a caution. The hotel is "in the islands, mon." The service is on island time; parts needed to make a repair, or even certain ingredients needed to prepare certain meals may have missed the boat today. Relax. Go with the flow, look around you, and just enjoy the view.

POISONOUS FRUITS
Some fruits and berries in the BVI are poisonous. Do not eat anything off a tree or bush unless you are absolutely sure you know what it is.

PUBLIC HOLIDAYS
Below are the major BVI holidays. Some float a bit, since they are tied to the moon or to something else that is floating. Banks and virtually all shops will be closed on these days. If a holiday falls on a Sunday, then count on the next Monday being a holiday, too. August Festival is actually two weeks of festivities. New Years Day; Commonwealth Day (2nd Monday in March); Good Friday; Easter Sunday; Easter Monday; Whit Monday (50 days after Easter); Sovereign's Birthday (June 11th); Territory Day (July 1st); Festival (ends with holidays 1st Monday-Wednesday in August); St. Ursula's Day(around October 21st); Christmas Day; Boxing Day (December 26th).

TAXIS
In the BVI, it is expected that passengers share taxis. When you are picked up at the airport or ferry, or even going into town from a resort, it is normal to share a taxi with people you don't know. Not only is this how the taxi driver can make a living, but it also enables a limited fleet of taxis to take everyone everywhere they need to go pretty much when they need to go there. (If three couples at the airport all waited for separate taxis, it would take much longer for many to get where they were going, since the same few taxis would be driving back and forth). An advantage to passengers is that you can all share information (where did you eat, what is it like where you are staying, etc.). If you are looking for a taxi in the middle of town and one goes by with or without passengers in it, call out your destination and the driver will stop, provided he or she is going that way. If you get a chance, talk to the drivers. Many have lived all over the world.

TELEPHONING AND CELL PHONES AND E-MAIL IN THE BVI

The area code for the BVI is 284 (which is easy to remember because it is BVI). When you are in the BVI, use the seven-digit telephone number. Lots of local establishments have cell phones (boat trips, taxi drivers, almost everyone on Jost Van Dyke) but they are sometimes "out of range" even though they aren't. Just try again later. Your stateside cell phone probably will not work in the BVI (ask your provider) but you can usually go to Cable & Wireless to get a connection for a fee. However, your cell phone often will still not work, so why not just relax and accept being "unconnected" for your trip (it actually can be delightful to be unreachable except in emergency; you can always be reached at your hotel or on a boat). For e-mail, see page 101.

TELEPHONING TO THE U.S. FROM THE BVI

There are several ways to call the US from the BVI, and sometimes none of them work. If you get stuck, just try again later. Dial 1-800-872-2881 for ATT (you can use your AT&T card or a major credit card) but sometimes this number will connect you with Cable & Wireless instead and you will only be able to use a major credit card. Dial 1-800-225-5872 or dial 111 or dial 191 and use a major credit card. Coin phone booths say you can dial long distance from them but you almost always can't (they often won't work locally with coins either).

TIME

The BVI is on Atlantic Standard Time, which is one hour ahead of Eastern Standard Time. However, the BVI does not switch to Daylight Savings Time and during these months the BVI are on the same time as U.S. eastern time.

WEATHER

Everyone tends to assume that the further south one goes, the hotter it is. Not true! The BVI daytime temperatures hover around 75 degrees in the winter, 85 degrees in the summer and the trade winds almost always blow. New York City can be much hotter in August than the BVI!

WHAT TO BRING

Sunscreen (the BVI are only 18 degrees from the equator and the sun is strong all year long), a little stick of bug repellant that you can keep in a pocket or purse, casual clothes. In the evening at the nicer restaurants on Tortola and Virgin Gorda, casual elegant resortwear is appropriate, including long pants and collared shirts for men. If you are staying on Jost Van Dyke, Anegada, or Cooper Island then you only need very casual clothes. Bring sturdy shoes if you want to hike and you might want a light sweater as evenings can be cool any time of year. You can always find a substitute but if you are particular about brands, bring enough shampoo, deodorant, etc.

FERRY SCHEDULES

Bear in mind that ferries can leave a little early or a little late. Also it is good advice to take the ferry that "looks like it is going soon" even if it is scheduled for a later departure than a ferry run by a competing company. For this reason, it makes sense to buy one-way rather than round-trip tickets.

BETWEEN TORTOLA AND JOST VAN DYKE

The ferry *Paradise Express* (495.9278) and the ferry *When* (494.2997) take 25-30 minutes to reach Great Harbor, Jost Van Dyke. The fare each way is $12. There is no ticket office. You pay on board. Just look for the boat, and be sure to get on when someone starts untying the lines. Departure time can be somewhat before or after the scheduled time. Sometimes on season on weekends or whenever enough people ask, there is a dinner ferry which leaves West End at 6:30 and returns later in the evening. Call if you're interested.

Schedule for the *Paradise Express*

From West End, Tortola	From Jost Van Dyke
9 am	7 am (Mon.-Fri)
10:30 am (Mon.-Fri)	8 am (Sat.-Sun.)
1 pm	9:30 (Mon.-Fri.)
3 pm	12 noon
6 pm	2 pm
	4:30 pm

Schedule for the *When*

From West End, Tortola	From Jost Van Dyke
7 am (Mon.-Sat.)	7:30 am (Mon.-Sat.)
8:15 am (Mon.-Sat.)	8:45 am (Mon.-Sat.)
9:30 am (Sun. only)	10:30 am
9:45 am (Mon.-Sat.)	12:45 pm
11:45 am	3 pm
1:30 pm	5 pm
4 pm	

BETWEEN TORTOLA AND COOPER ISLAND

Extremely limited ferry service runs between Cooper Island and Prospect Reef Marina just outside of Road Town, Tortola. Schedules are subject to change, so please call (*495.9084*). Fare is $15 each way.

Monday-Friday

From Cooper	From Prospect Reef
7 am	8:30 am
4:30 pm	5:30 pm

BETWEEN TORTOLA AND VIRGIN GORDA (THE VALLEY)

In Tortola, ferries leave from the ferry docks in Road Town (across from Pusser's). In The Valley, ferries leave from the public dock just north (and within walking distance) of the Virgin Gorda Yacht Harbour. The fare is $10 each way and takes about 35 minutes. Times are daily unless noted.

on SPEEDY'S FERRIES (495-5240)

From Virgin Gorda	From Road Town
6:30 am (Tues., Thurs.)	9 am
8 am	10:10 am (Tues., Thurs.)
10 am	10:30 am
11:30 am	12 noon
12:30 am	1:30 pm
2:45 pm (Tues., Thurs.)	4:30 pm
3:30 pm	5:15 pm (Sun.)
4:30 pm (Sun.)	6 pm (Mon. Wed., Fri.)
5 pm (Mon., Wed., Fri.)	6:15 pm (Tues., Thurs.)
6 pm (Wed., Sat.)	6:45 pm (Wed., Sat.)
10:30 pm (Wed., Sat.)	11 pm (Wed., Sat.)

on SMITH'S FERRIES (495-4495)

From Road Town	From Virgin Gorda
7 am (Mon-Sat)	7:50 am (Mon-Sat)
8:50 am	10:15 am
12:30 pm	2:15 pm (Mon.-Fri.)
3:15 pm (Mon-Fri)	3 pm (Sat.-Sun.)
4:15 (Sat, Sun)	4 pm (Mon.-Fri.)
	5 pm (Sat.-Sun.)

BETWEEN TORTOLA AND VIRGIN GORDA

The **North Sound Express** (*495-2138*) runs between Trellis Bay (on Beef Island past the airport) and the Bitter End Yacht Club on North Sound. The trip takes 30 minutes (45 if there is a stop at the Valley) and is $40 round-trip. Advance reservations are absolutely essential and departure times are subject to change, particularly from the Valley. (The Valley and Bitter End have no ticket offices. Stand at the end of the dock to be sure the pilot sees you at these departures.)

From Tortola/Beef Island	From the Valley	From North Sound
8:15 am	8:30 am	6:45 am
11:15 am	11:30 am	9 am
1 pm	4 pm	12 noon
3:45 pm	5:45 pm	2:45 pm
5:30 pm		4:30 pm
7:30 pm ($25 one-way)		6:15 pm

139

BETWEEN TORTOLA AND MARINA CAY

The trip takes about 10 minutes and is free. Ferries leave from the little dock near the Trellis Bay Market which is a bit east of the Beef Island airport.

From Beef Island	From Marina Cay
10:30 am	10:15 am
11:30 am	11:15 am
12:30 pm	12:15 pm
3:00 pm	2:45 pm
4:00 pm	3:45 pm
5:00 pm	4:45 pm
6:00 pm	5:45 pm
7:00 pm	6:45 pm
	7:45 pm (for restaurant guests)
	8:45 pm (for restaurants guests)

BETWEEN TORTOLA AND PETER ISLAND

The trip takes about 30 minutes. Ferries leave from the resort's private dock, which many still call the CSY Dock, which is ten minutes outside of Road Town, on the east side of Road Town Harbour. The fare is $15.00 per person. Fares are waived for those who have dinner reservations at Peter Island.

From Road Town	From Peter Island
7:00 am	8:00 am
8:30 am	9:00 am
10:00 am	11:30 am
12 noon	1:30 pm
2:00 pm	2:30 pm
3:30 pm	4:30 pm
5:30 pm	6:00 pm
6:30 pm	7:30 pm
8:00 pm	10:00 pm
10:30 pm	11:30 pm

BETWEEN GUN CREEK, VIRGIN GORDA AND THE BITTER END YACHT CLUB (NORTH SOUND, VIRGIN GORDA)

The trip takes about 10 minutes and is free. At Gun Creek, the little wooden Bitter End ferry leaves from the dock. You can grab a beer or a soda from the Last Stop Bar across the street. And don't worry if there's not a soul around or a boat in sight. The ferry will appear! The ferry leaves Gun Creek every hour on the 1/2 hour beginning at 6:30 am and ending at 10:30 pm. The ferry leaves Bitter End every hour on the hour beginning at 6 am and ending at 11 pm.

INDEX

INDEX

ABOUT THE AUTHOR

Pamela Acheson was Vice-President and Director of Marketing for a Fortune-500 publishing company in New York City until she and her husband headed south over a decade ago. Since their successful escape she has lived in, explored, and written extensively about Florida and the Caribbean.

In addition to being the author of *The Best of the British Virgin Islands*, Ms. Acheson is the co-author (with her husband Richard B. Myers) of *The Best of St. Thomas and St. John, U.S. Virgin Islands* and *The Best Romantic Escapes in Florida, Volume One* and *The Best Romantic Escapes in Florida, Volume Two*.

In addition to her own books and consulting, Ms. Acheson has contributed to many guide books including *Fodor's Caribbean*, *Fodor's Virgin Islands*, *Fodor's Florida*, *Fodor's Walt Disney World*, and *Fodor's Cruises and Ports of Call.*

Her articles and photographs have appeared in numerous publications including *Travel and Leisure*, *Caribbean Travel and Life*, and *Florida Travel and Life*. She lives and travels in Florida and the Virgin Islands with her husband.